The Bellbind Letters

THE BELLBIND LETTERS

Inside the Devil's Plan for Your Motherhood

SAMANTHA N. STEPHENSON

Nihil Obstat
Msgr. Michael Heintz, Ph.D.
Censor Librorum

Imprimatur
✠Kevin C. Rhoades
Bishop of Fort Wayne-South Bend
September 17, 2025

The *Nihil Obstat* and *Imprimatur* are official declarations that a book is free from doctrinal or moral error. It is not implied that those who have granted the *Nihil Obstat* and *Imprimatur* agree with the contents, opinions, or statements expressed.

31 30 29 28 27 26 1 2 3 4 5 6 7 8 9

Our Sunday Visitor Publishing Division
Our Sunday Visitor, Inc., 200 Noll Plaza, Huntington, IN 46750; www.osv.com; 1-800-348-2440.

ISBN: 978-1-63966-329-3 (Inventory No. T2971)

1. RELIGION—Christian Living—Women's Interests.
2. RELIGION—Christian Living—Spiritual Warfare.
3. RELIGION—Christianity—Catholic.

eISBN: 978-1-63966-330-9
LCCN: 2025948624

Cover design: Tyler Ottinger
Interior design: Amanda Falk
Cover art: AdobeStock

PRINTED IN THE UNITED STATES OF AMERICA

For Garrett,
who unceasingly mirrors the merciful
love of Jesus Christ in my life.

For our children,
may we always do the same for you.

For the mothers of the Treasure
Valley Catholic community,
whose dedication to faithful
motherhood inspires my own.

And for Mary, Mother of God,
who reveals to us all the
meaning of motherhood.

Contents

There are two equal and opposite errors into which our race can fall about the devils. One is to disbelieve their existence. The other is to believe, and to feel an excessive and unhealthy interest in them. They themselves are equally pleased with both errors and hail a materialist or a magician with the same delight.

Readers are advised to remember that the devil is a liar. Not everything that Screwtape says should be assumed to be true even from his own angle.

There is wishful thinking in Hell as well as on Earth.

— C. S. Lewis, *The Screwtape Letters*, Introduction

Before Anything Else

My husband and I reread C. S. Lewis's *The Screwtape Letters* every Lent — that is, when Screwtape doesn't get the best of us. Screwtape, the imaginary tempter whose letters comprise the book, has become an integral part of our spiritual language as a couple. When we hear in the other's words petty judgments, pharisaical preoccupations, or a general failure to receive reality with gratitude, we might say to each other, "I think that's Screwtape talking."

There is a reason why this literary classic has been a bestseller in Christian and secular categories alike since its publication (as I write, it is the #1 bestseller in Christian Classics on Amazon). Best known for his children's Christian allegory *The Chronicles of Narnia* and apologetics texts such as *Mere Christianity*, Lewis is the author of over thirty books, including the narrative Christian fiction *The Great Divorce* and the satirical epistolary novel *The Screwtape Letters*.[1] It is these latter two that demonstrate that Lewis's psychological genius matched his theological prowess; Lewis painted the nature of our human brokenness with an eerily accurate brush.

Helpful Hints

For those who are unfamiliar with the work in question and those who may need a bit of a refresher, allow me to briefly explain that *The Screwtape Letters* unfolds through a series of one-sided letters in which a senior demon, Screwtape, mentors a younger demon in the art of temptation. Through Screwtape's letters, we receive the story of a newly converted young man and his struggles to live the Christian life virtuously. This character, termed "the patient" by his tempters, stands in the place of us all. Readers cringe and shudder in awe at the accuracy with which Lewis manages to depict the interior battle between virtue and vice that rages within. Because Lewis writes from the perspective of the demonic, everything in his letters (and the letters that follow in this book) is reversed. Satan becomes "Our Father Below" and God the Father is referred to as "the Enemy."

The Bellbind Letters mimic Lewis in structure and style. Fans of the original will note that these letters are written not to Wormwood but to a new underde-

1. "C. S. Lewis: The Should've-Been-a-Catholic Apologist." Catholic.com, https://www.catholic.com/magazine/print-edition/c-s-lewis-the-shouldve-been-a-catholic-apologist.

mon, Bellbind — as Wormwood (spoiler alert) perished graphically after his failure to secure his patient's soul for the underworld — and that the senior demon in question is no longer Screwtape, but Boomslang. Unlike Lewis's newly converted Christian, the "patient" in these pages is a Catholic mother striving — imperfectly — to live a holy life. As in the original Lewis, we receive a single side of the correspondence, much like we would if we stumbled upon Bellbind's stash secreted away. Though it is Boomslang's voice we hear in these pages, Bellbind is the twisted tempter intervening in this patient's life to lure her to hell. These letters, though not written by another, comprise the methods this demon employs; thus, Bellbind becomes the titular character, as the primary figure luring the patient away from Christ.

The Genius of Screwtape

The genius of Lewis's satirical strategy lies in the power of art and literature to pierce the heart. Screwtape's diabolical reversal is a disarming mirror that allows us to see the depth of perversion lurking in even the simplest of temptations and most minor of vices.

Those who feel a certain squeamishness in reading a narrative that takes the perspective of the demonic show a good impulse; better to be cautious than to deny the existence of these evil forces altogether. Bishop Robert Barron reassures readers of *The Screwtape Letters*: "What gives Lewis the confidence to mock the devil is his confidence that Christ has already won this great battle."[2] In other words, even the methods of evil themselves, illuminated by the light of Christ, can be used as instruments for God's good purposes. In this case, they do so by enlightening us about the twisted ways we deceive ourselves and the pitfalls of pride that lurk around every corner of Christian life.

In the nearly 100 years since its publication, *The Screwtape Letters* has become a popular object of elaboration and emulation. There are modern translations, study guides, dramatizations — even a version about pickleball! In the Catholic world, writer Emily Stimpson Chapman once gave a talk called "Screwtape's Snare," and author Elizabeth Scalia offered a critique of contemporary American culture via Screwtape's voice at Word on Fire.[3] In the same year that I penned this manuscript, Catholic speaker Emily Wilson and evangelical writer Tilley Dillehay were at work on book-length imitations of their own. The esteemed philosopher Peter Kreeft called his iteration, *The Snakebite Letters*, "a shameless plagiarism," defending the genre of imitations thus: "I have no shame about it, because I'm sure Lewis wanted such 'plagiarisms.'"[4] If anything, the genre appears to be gaining momentum as time passes.

My first foray into the Screwtape Imitation Club was

---

2. "Bishop Robert Barron on C. S. Lewis." YouTube. Uploaded Nov. 20, 2013. https://www.youtube.com/watch?v=dlQuYXtkx0g

3. "Uncle Screwtape Is Delighted with Our Social Cowardice." Word on Fire, https://www.wordonfire.org/articles/fellows/uncle-screwtape-is-delighted-with-our-social-cowardice/.

4. Kreeft, Peter. *The Snakebite Letters: Devilishly Devious Secrets for Subverting Society as Taught in Tempter's Training School.* Ignatius Press, 1998, 7.

in 2021, when I was invited to write a testimony for the Idaho Catholic Women's Conference. When all the reasons I put to paper rang trite, I found it much easier to articulate all the reasons for women not to attend. As Screwtape's diabolical purposes came to light, the reasons in favor of attending shined all the more brightly. A reworked version of my original letter appears as Letter 4 of this book.

As the idea for this reimagining took root in my mind and began branching out into different spheres of my life, I became enchanted by this new way of seeing reality. Recognizing how effective my own faults and failings were at deterring me from living out Christ's generosity was revolutionary; the mere knowledge of their concrete manifestations was itself a powerful tool for resisting these pervasive temptations. As the list of notes on my phone grew, my conviction that I was to share these insights deepened. Each time I heard another mother echo similar struggles, I recognized what a balm and fortification this book might provide. The moment the fact of the project became real, however, Screwtape began whispering in the back of my mind: "What makes you think your writing could ever come close to Lewis's? How arrogant and silly to even make the attempt."

Fortunately, I am as well acquainted with G. K. Chesterton as I am with impostor syndrome, so I was able to answer back, "If a thing is worth doing, it is worth doing badly."[5] Even cakes made with imitation vanilla, though they may lack the richness of the real deal, are still worth tasting. It is in this spirit that I offer you my own pale imitation of Lewis on the following pages.

It should also be noted that, for all his brilliance, Lewis never formally converted to Catholicism (nobody's perfect!). In that regard, what this author lacks by way of Lewis's psychological brilliance, she makes up for in access to the fullness of Truth as communicated via the Magisterium. Where Lewis occupied himself primarily with those truths common to "mere Christianity," I have at my disposal the splendor of the Truth as revealed in Scripture and Tradition and interpreted by the Magisterium under the guidance of the Holy Spirit to draw from in my offering to Lewis's literary legacy. To my knowledge, the book you hold in your hands is the only "shameless plagiarism" to date where you'll find the Mass, the Eucharist, Confession, and Our Lady taking center stage — described, of course, in all their "despicable filth" (as the demons would say).

Do Moms Need Screwtape?

Although *The Screwtape Letters* as a work of literary genius is truly unrepeatable, more can be said on the nature and specificity of temptations as they manifest in the lives of contemporary women, mothers especially. This book seeks to emulate Lewis's rhetorical brilliance in order to highlight the temptations Christian mothers

5. Chesterton, G. K. *What's Wrong with the World.* Cassell and Co., 1910.

face on the road to sanctity. Women have been uniquely gifted by our Creator, instilled with the feminine genius; it only stands to reason that the temptations to stray from this unique God-given identity will manifest themselves as a particular and specific attack against it.

In the following pages, we will delve into an examination of conscience, guided by the wily words of Boomslang, to uncover the subtle temptations that we face in our daily lives. This demon's twisted logic provides insight into our deepest temptations that paradoxically aid us in discerning the voice of God amidst the cacophony of life.

How to Read This Book

Familiarity with Lewis's work is by no means a prerequisite for reading this book. *The Bellbind Letters* provides a way for devotees of Lewis's classic to dive deeper into spiritual reflection that resonates even more clearly with their everyday lives, while also being accessible to those who have never before heard the name of Screwtape. While reading, allow yourself to be challenged and transformed as you unmask your everyday temptations. Scripture tells us to be on alert: "Your adversary the devil prowls around like a roaring lion, seeking someone to devour," (1 Peter 5:8).[6] Recognizing our temptations doesn't mean that we always have the fortitude or prudence to choose the better path, but seeing ourselves

6. Revised Standard Version, Second Catholic Edition. Ascension Publishing, LLC, 2018.

clearly allows us to take the first step.

Anthony de Mello writes that to love a thing means "to see a person, a thing, a situation, as it really is and not as you imagine it to be, and to give it the response it deserves. You cannot love what you do not even see."[7] It can be quite difficult to see ourselves clearly, especially when it requires a good, long look at those parts of ourselves that we would rather stay hidden. Putting on the narrative lens of the demonic tempter provides just enough distance for us to see ourselves reflected clearly in the trials and temptations of the mother, "the patient" in the story. Remember that all is seen in reverse, through demonic inversion; and so just as what gives the demons glee should alert us to spiritual danger, what causes them fear and revulsion appears all the more precious to us.

As you read, take note of what stirs within you. No doubt you will recognize the tendencies described in yourself, in family and friends, in neighbors and strangers alike. Resist the urge to accuse or despair. That is merely our pal Bellbind talking. Our sinful condition is the tragic byproduct of our fallen nature, but the good news of the Gospel is that the story doesn't end there! My hope is that women will use the following pages as an examination of conscience that will illuminate the shadowy places of our lives. Use the discussion guide in the Appendix to deepen your

7. De Mello, Anthony. *The Way to Love: The Last Meditations of Anthony De Mello.* Image, 1995.

reflection and steer your discussions (a free printable download, complete with study guide and journal pages, is available at www.snstephenson.com/bellbind). In the end, it is seeing ourselves clearly, in all our weaknesses and failings, that frees us to respond with the love de Mello describes — to surrender all our broken pieces to the tender mercy of Christ the healer, who makes all things new.

1
On Snatching Souls

My Dear Bellbind,

What a pleasure it is to hear from you. I must thank you for your kind condolences on the loss of my former protégé's patient. In point of fact, he slipped right out of the incompetent Datura's meager grasp and fell to prey to the Enemy's infernal mercy. What an intolerable invention! The whole incident is entirely regrettable and could have been avoided had the patient not been assigned such a useless tempter.

You and I shall no doubt prove more effective in our efforts with your patient. I understand that you are troubled by her relationship with the Enemy at present. And it is true that His so-called Sacraments, dripping as they are with that disgusting material filth polluting his infernal grace, do provide certain fortifications against our efforts.

You must not fret. Patients of her ilk are just as easily lured in Our Father's direction, though they require an entirely different sort of bait. It is no large matter. I shall instruct you presently in the art of illusion and frivolity. There is much we can do with a soul in her condition, and though it may take some doing, a slow and steady effort can lull even the most devout of souls into indifference and tarnish any resemblance she might now bear to that most hideous of images.

I understand the pain you experience now while in her presence; that will soon subside as we take care to dim the light of the Enemy's aura so that her company might be less blinding.

While it is true that patients who manage to reach such levels of effulgence tend to stay their course, do not despair. Our cause is not lost. There is a special kind of sweetness about the business of luring a blazing soul into the waters of tepidity. It will require a full wearing down of her fervor, endless distractions and worldliness, fanning of old resentments, and bolstering of any lingering pride — in short, anything that makes her forget her love of the Enemy, even for the smallest moment. We can seize on those occasions and encourage their growth, minute as such growth may be in the beginning. Like our friend the cancer, we must eat away at her slowly and imperceptibly to start, so that our dominion over her may go undetected as long as possible — ideally, until she meets her grave, having surrendered her soul to our perversions bit by bit, until no more is left to will the contrary.

All this is to say that yes, I do think it is entirely possible to accomplish Our Father's designs for her, but by no means will this be a simple task. Remember Wormwood, a tempter whose patient was far newer to the Enemy's fold than yours, yet whose failure to capture his patient's soul left us no choice but to devour him. And so, I caution you to remain mindful of the torments that await us all should we fail in service to Our Father Below.

I cannot but stress to you the precarious nature of her soul, given her affections for things tainted by His presence. It is urgent that we use every means possible to separate her from the habitual actions that stoke these affections. It is no use to attack the affections merely for a soul in her condition. One such as she is likely to persist in her habits, no matter how dry or wearisome they become. Much safer to impose impediments that undermine these infernal habits themselves. Break the habits and the behavior will alter. Change the behavior and the affections will drift away like mists on the waters: slowly, silently, and without occasion.

With love and venom,
Boomslang

2
On Prayer

My Dear Bellbind,

How pleased I am to hear that you have begun your attack on the patient's habit of prayer. As you well know, His voice is quite fuzzy to us, but the humans are entirely susceptible. Even the slightest raising of their consciousness to Him can have disastrous consequences for our grasp on their meager wills. The slightest and most tepid of souls have been steeled against us by the mere raising of hearts and mind to the Enemy. It follows that *anything* you can do to undermine the habit of prayer is of great use to us. It does little good to provide a momentary interruption, or even distract with a week's worth of terrible illness, unless you can break the patient of her *habit* of seeking Him out, for He is always ready to receive her.

On that note, a nasty illness can be a dangerous business in this regard, and I advise you to avoid producing it unless you are certain of how your patient will respond. Pain and suffering must be applied just so. One misstep and you'll have your patient rushing back into the Enemy's loathsome caress. Reminding the humans of their fragility can produce the distasteful effect of humility, and is there anything more revolting than a soul that knows its own littleness? Puffed up is what we want! Pride produces a barrier such that little can pass through. Why, it might even be made of material filth, solid as its effects are at blocking the flow of the Enemy's infernal graces. As it is, we can be grateful it belongs to the spiritual realm and makes such a useful tool when properly wielded.

But back to the subject of habit breaking. Habits are entirely galling in our work precisely because we can make so little headway when they are in place. They are like a furrow produced by their wheelbarrows, creating such a divot. At first, the wheel easily veers off course. (If we can catch a soul in this stage, our work is made simple.) But, by the gradual wearing down of the same path repeatedly, day after day, the furrow deepens, the path becomes its own constraint, and the wheel cannot deviate from its course except by some great outside force that overcomes it.

The only solace to be had is that *any* behavior can be turned to habit, and so we must both prevent the digging of paths that lead toward the Enemy while simultaneously encouraging the slow but steady furrowing of paths that lead to Our Father Below. As we instruct all our novice tempters, so I remind you: *The safest path to Hell is the gradual one.* No need to engage the patient in grave sin if mere distractions will do. After all, grave sin, as deliciously as it covers the stench of an otherwise pure soul, carries with it the danger of awakening the patient to the dire state of her soul. The key is to lure *gradually,* so that the patient does not notice the deepening of the grooves, even when they become high walls that have all but removed her freedom to walk any other way.

Since the invention of screens, much of our work in the area of distraction has become automated. Truth be told, even our best had struggled somewhat after the War, when many humans finally recognized the depravity of evils we produced in working up their bloodlust. So many souls were lost to us by the turning of the conscience — nasty little loophole the Enemy has implanted in them. You see what I mean about grave sin? Entirely too dangerous until we have worn the furrow walls so high that the patient in question can no longer see over them, no longer see anything at all but blackness, so that as she travels the well-worn path of sin, she sees no other path and indeed feels most comfortable traversing it.

The screens, you see, carry in them any manner of distraction. The delightful thing of it is that these distractions can even be what the Enemy's closest friends call "good." You can feed your patient any number of inputs, and they can even be directly about prayer or motherhood or any of the sort of things that will make her feel that her time has been edifying and well spent.

I once stoked a female to spill over in outrage at the interruption of her real children, requiring her attention at just the moment she was immersed in reading some quotation or another on the meaning of motherhood. The key is that it serves as a distraction. And true, something here or there may spark the sting of conscience, but that is easily remedied; merely douse it with a flood of indignance and you'll have her stewing over that all day. It is most unlikely, even when the steady stream of content is *about* the Enemy himself, that any of it will lead your patient to raise her consciousness *to* the Enemy, and that is the only real danger. You may worry if the content the patient is consuming fills her with a steady diet of the true and beautiful. No matter, I tell you — so long as you can veer the patient off course, lead her to neglect her family, her present duty, and the presence of the Enemy himself.

With love and venom,
Boomslang

3
On Screens

My Dear Bellbind,

I am pleased to hear what headway you have made immersing your patient in the world of screens. What a triumph you have had in convincing her that her time is best spent documenting her family's activities and magnanimously offering her sage advice to other mothers. You are right to be concerned about the possibility that she may eventually wake up to the ways she is neglecting her family to attend to what is essentially an ego-boosting activity. In the event that this occurs, you will need to rely on the addictive mechanisms the humans have built into these technologies for us.

To be sure, it is still safer should she never realize the ways in which her children have been left hungering for her attention, but sweet torment lies ahead if awareness finally dawns. Augment in her mind the pain and loneliness she has inflicted, and make her cognizant of how quickly time is passing (this is never a fact to highlight when it might cause her to *treasure* the time she has proactively, mind you; only make her aware of it in the *past* tense, as something that is gone, that she has allowed to slip through her fingers, never to be seen again). If you time it carefully, you will be able to ease off just as resolve begins to take hold, at which point you must switch gears (we would never want her to change behavior *in actuality*). We want her to feel the pangs of regret to the point of self-loathing, whilst never admitting to herself the possibility of real change. This is where the addiction proves so useful to us.

Just at the moment when she leans into giving herself to her children, her husband, or any other task that the Enemy has set out for her, you must make her feel the full weight of the *tedium* of the moment. If you can stir up any lingering resentments or difficulties in the behavior of the children, all the better. The key is to put her in such a state as to long for an escape. Misery is preferable but mere boredom will do — so long as she turns her attention away from the moment and back into the endless stream of the screen.

With love and venom,
Boomslang

4
On Rest

My Dear Bellbind,

You did the right thing in confiding to me your patient's impulse to attend the retreat. The key here is to redirect her desire to refresh her soul toward something far less sustaining. Can you convince the patient that her spiritual dryness is due to overwork? That she is altogether too busy and rundown to exert herself in attendance of this sudden extraneous obligation? It is of no consequence that it is exactly this sort of thing that might truly refresh her; our aim must be to obscure that fact completely, keeping it from the patient's conscious realization.

This is most efficiently achieved by distraction, and such distraction is most delectable to us when it consists not of true pleasure, but rather of turmoil. Stir up false guilt of every kind. Remind her that her husband and family cannot do without her. Entice her into believing her presence in her home is indispensable.

You must encourage her pride in such a way that she maintains the image of herself as self-sacrificial mother, one who gives at every moment and takes nothing for herself. This image of mother is one of our better inventions, as it preys on a woman's natural inclinations toward self-gift, twisting them into imitation martyrdom. In this condition, mothers are driven to pour out everything they have and are easily lured away from anything that might refresh or refill them for fear of being perceived as "selfish." This fear is an opportunity; use it to prevent your patient from approaching anything that might truly quench her soul.

You are right to fear this retreat. Any refreshment of the soul at regular intervals provides a steady obstacle to our goals for it; a whole heap of it at once may prove difficult for us to overcome indeed. Our aim, of course, is the gradual and nearly imperceptible drying out of your patient's soul. As she becomes brittle, having avoided nourishment and rest, she is less able to perceive the Enemy's insipid plan for her existence and eternal significance. Once you have led her to this state, little further effort from you will be required. Any small irritation or inconvenience may be enough to trigger a snap, provided you have cultivated a gradual buildup of resentment against the very ones she has been designed to nurture. Thus, your patient will herself erode the bonds of love with those whom you have convinced her that she cannot leave.

In this way, my twisted deceiver, the patient will slowly but surely starve her soul, leaving to the side the riches the Enemy has prepared for her, until it exists on nothing but the worldly platitudes we have planted in the culture at large. Once you have drawn her into abandoning by habit those things she once clung to as necessary for her immortal soul, you can begin once again to coax her into absence from her dear ones, provided that the sustenance she seeks is nothing truly satisfying: a pedicure, a bubble bath — anything will do, provided that it is spiritually shallow in nature and conducted under the intention to escape from these wretched, draining creatures.

So you see, you must wait for the moment your patient has withdrawn her affections and begun to foster the resentment that we once had to suggest to her. Only then is it safe to allow her to believe that she ought to withdraw physically: when the cause is some superficial act of "self-care" and nothing that might truly feed her emaciated spirit.

With love and venom,
Boomslang

5
On Consumerism

My Dear Bellbind,

It is truly regrettable that the patient has chosen to attend the retreat. Now is the time to tread lightly. She has made up her mind; there is no deterring her attendance in body, but you may yet have some hope for her soul. The key is to ensure that her physical presence affects nothing whatsoever of her interior life. True, she may experience something of the fervor that the Enemy likes to offer His children as an enticement to remain at His side. But these feelings can be turned to advantage by a skilled tempter. The patient must be made to value the experience of this sweetness (and they do experience it as sweetness, however despicable it may be to us) as the end in itself. In other words, do not allow her to see it for what it is, a byproduct of proximity to the Enemy and not the Enemy Himself. That way, when He inevitably withdraws His infernal bribery, your patient will feel the loss so sharply that her only point of focus will be her own pain. It is the patients who continue on in their pursuit of the Enemy in lieu of any tangible consolations that venture into realms beyond our reach.

In the meantime, we have a veritable treasure trove of time-tested strategies to dull your patient's religious impulses and render her inert. If, in hearing these so-called testimonies they rattle off at the retreat, your patient is struck or taken in by this particular point or that, encourage a fixation on that point. Take care here; *true* engagement with the promotions may amount to cooperation with the Enemy and acceptance of His graces. We can't have that. The best we can hope for in these circumstances is to convict the patient of the illusion that she must improve this or that spiritual imperfection by her own power. Better still if we can stir up shame and dissatisfaction with what is ultimately nothing more than her natural limitations as a creature and not a god in herself. In this way, you will find that we can elicit a kind of pride that manifests itself as self-deprecation, maybe even self-hatred. So long as it keeps the patient despairing of the status of her soul, ashamed to approach the Enemy, despising her own helplessness, we can rejoice in watching her weave herself captive in a cage of her own creation.

If she will not be lured into forms of outright despair or the Sisyphean trap of making herself into her own savior, you may well succeed with distraction. Nothing overt, as you want to take care to avoid those temptations to which the patient herself has deep aversions. Instead, you must cloak your distractions in pious disguise so that she may mistake them for religious impulse. Exploit human proclivity for the amassing of things. Lead her to linger over the marketplace, and she may well convince herself that she is doing as much good leafing through baubles and trivialities as she would in the chapel gazing at the Enemy or fingering That Woman's blasted chain of beaded filth. Oh, I know that we shudder to gaze upon these images, but as the Enemy has seen fit to make the infernal flesh bags so dependent upon their senses for knowledge of the world, we may as well turn that to our advantage. It matters not what foul dangers these items are to us; the key is to convince the patient that she cannot live without them, and that, indeed, her very salvation depends upon their acquisition.

The more you can clutter up her mind toward the amassing of various books, pious plastic, and devotional trinkets, the less space she will have for those things that pose a real threat. She must accumulate but never employ! The less stillness and silence you allow her, the smaller the chance of her raising heart and mind to the Enemy's advances. We know that He is such a coward that He awaits their invitation. Can you imagine? There is, and never has been, any accounting for His utter foolishness. Thankfully, Our Father Below has no such qualms and so, where invitation may be lacking, he still advances wherever Enemy lines prove weak. It matters not whether she fills her bag with statues of ragtag vagabonds or pithy stickers — so long as her mind is consumed with filling the bag and not her soul.

Your efforts to prevent the patient from prayerful postures of the heart will prove profitable if, upon her return home, you exploit the habit you have planted — and through the very items purported to be in service of the Enemy, no less! This will be even easier when she is removed from that loathsome environment filled with so many barriers to us, reeking of the stench of filthy virtues and the straining sound of voices offered in wretched, mewling praising of the Enemy and His armies.

Yes, when she returns, we will again have the use of an indispensable tool in our current endeavor: the advertisement. We have always been able to agitate souls via comparison, to lead them to consider the possessions, circumstances, and gifts of others, until they, like Cain, are dripping with delectable envy. If you are very fortunate, you may one day have the ease of tempting a hot-headed patient like Cain, so prone to anger that he can be stoked into murderous rage. Your patient is far more possessed of virtue, but we may conquer her yet.

Whether she comes home stinking of consolations or you successfully lure her into an altogether shallow collecting of gaudy, saccharine baubles, she will inevitably come down from what they term the "mountaintop" experience. When her family is vexing her and all is commonplace and ordinary, things will lose their shine. The patient will experience the aridity that is merely a fact of human life. You must seize upon this moment. Make her despair of what is an altogether normal human experience. Insist that the incongruity between the lofty feelings of religious fervor and the lowly life she leads is due to deficiencies inherent to her mission. She must never suspect the Enemy's intention lurking in the ordinary. What a fool He is! We have merely to emphasize the dullness of what He asks of her. Humans almost always fall for a program of habitual dissatisfaction — and no wonder. What kind of all-powerful Being expects His subjects to be wooed by invitations to putrid simplicity and groveling humility! The imbecile really does much of the work for us, honestly. Had He added any real pizzaz or sparkle, we might have a challenge, but *ordinary*? Ha! Little enchantment there when we can spin them about with the delights and pleasures Our Father Below has rightfully commandeered from the Enemy's own hands to seduce them!

Whisper to her about the longings in the depths of her soul and teach her to see how utterly insufficient those in her life are to satisfy them. This should be fairly straightforward; we know that the Enemy has placed these yearnings there to lead her on this search. This is where we come in. We must befuddle His plans for the humans to seek Him out. What they don't know can most certainly be made to hurt them. You see, they are so forgetful that even those who *do* realize that this longing is meant to lead them to the Enemy can be made to chase after any number of ridiculous pursuits. The key is to keep them running.

Stir up her voracious appetites for any manner of lesser goods, and you will successfully redirect her impulses. This is where advertising comes so in handy. Whereas we used to be limited by the proximity of their social betters to elicit dissatisfaction at what they lack and eliminate gratitude for what they do possess, now no such proximity is required. Patients like yours are in a state of near-constant exposure to all that they do not have. The actual items they long for matter not. They can be made to spend, spend, spend on the latest fashions, convenience in the kitchen, or even books about the Enemy himself (though, as a rule, these should generally be avoided in all but the most desperate of circumstances). Naturally, the more trivial and devoid of meaning, the more surely this path will lead to Our Father Below. But the items themselves matter relatively little, so long as you can lead your patient in a continual cycle of amassing what she does not already have.

Why, just the other day I found myself congratulating our colleague Melandra on crafting a hamster wheel of sorts on which his patient's mind daily trots in a cycle of online searching, selecting, overspending, shaming, and returning. She added this last step for herself upon finding that she was drowning in debt, which might be taken as a sign of contrition if it weren't for the fact that she never falters off the wheel. She trots along, and, if ever her eyes seem to deviate from the pursuit of the next prize, Melandra merely reminds her of the rush of acquisition and the delight of opening the next postman's parcel. Cloud over the trough in her mind; so long as they fixate on the high, they will trot on.

Whatever fails to satisfy will do the trick (and, as nothing but the Enemy Himself will do so, we are at extreme advantage on this point). The key to this technique is this: Lead her as far down the rabbit hole as she will go, enticing her to waste much of her material wealth and precious time pursuing these possessions while obscuring her understanding of what she truly desires. I must underscore that what we are after here is primarily her *time*, as you will no doubt recognize from my illustration of Melandra's hamster wheel. The crippling debt and the ensuing shame are lovely toppings, to be sure, but the sweet substance of the thing is to suck her soul into a chasm of nothingness; little accomplishes this so well as the occupation of her mind, moment by moment, with triviality and unreality. The more time you manage to occupy, the safer she is from pursuing any manner of the dangers the Enemy has littered about the landscape of her life to entice her to His purposes. Thankfully, the damnable little creature's vision is dim at best, and her ability to distinguish what is of worth (according to His perverse purposes) dimmer still.

Exploit her natural rewards to trigger a near addiction to obtaining things, and she may well be led to spend far beyond her means or even to hide her purchases from her spouse and deliberately deceive him about her spending habits. If you can train her to these more deadly habits, it will be all the more delicious for you. And no, it does not matter that eventually, her interests in amassing the items du jour will wane; you must count on it. We need merely to pivot her to the next preoccupation. One rabbit hole is as good as another, provided that it does not lead to direct contact with the Enemy Himself. Your mantra must be this: spend, consume, obtain, hoard. Those souls who can be made to scurry on the hamster wheel of consumerism make delightful pets, running on and on, failing to notice that their efforts take them nowhere. We must keep them panting, waiting, exhausted, and entirely blinded to the Enemy's banquet lest they grow wise to the satisfaction that awaits them should they only pause long enough to step off.

With love and venom,
Boomslang

6
On Vanity

My Dear Bellbind,

I am encouraged to hear that you have been making such progress fanning the flames of the patient's avarice. Undoubtedly, she will find herself consumed by her own voracious appetite for things; the more that she amasses, the less will remain of herself, until she shrivels into nothingness. You must take care to continually present the things she *must have* in varying categories, else she will grow wise to your tactics and, having amassed such a large quantity of items in any one category, will grow weary of the whole endeavor. In a sense, this is precisely what we wish: Tempting is all the sweeter when, instead of reveling in natural pleasures imbued by the Enemy, you can draw a soul even further into the drab grayness of dull materialism. In keeping your patient preoccupied with what she can touch, feel, taste, consume, you close her mind to the pleasures of the spiritual realm. If you can habituate her to her flesh cage, soon she will lose the sense that she can and ought to raise her mind above what is laid before her. Tempters who are successful in our program of habitual satisfaction of their patient's basest desires breed dull, senseless pets who look forward to nothing but an endless cycle of want and satisfaction.

In tempting a patient of the female sort, it is always useful to prey upon her concerns with the arrangement of her flesh. Oh, the Enemy has indeed made them for Beauty, but we can seize upon their impulses toward it, and twist to our own delectable ends. Convince her that the beauty she longs for is not to be found in the transcendent realm of the Enemy but is some fixed quality of the material realm that is continually slipping through her grasp. Never allow her to think of what is eternal or unseen, but only that which is visible. Her mind must be made to fixate on earthly forms of beauty; distorted forms are best. Let her not consider the transitory nature of her life nor the fleeting essence of a glimmer of beauty she recognizes in her own reflection. Let her think not of the Enemy's purposes for it — and certainly not that this transience is, as the despicable little meat bags say, a feature, not a bug, intended for her own sanctification — but only of what she may gain by turning it toward her own immediate gratification.

Entice her to a consumerism of the body, to primp and polish her hair and her skin. Let her fixate on the smallest of her imperfections, and she will naturally begin to despair the lines in her eyes, forehead, and mouth. Never mind that these have been etched there by many years of reveling in the gifts of the Enemy; even these can be turned to our advantage if the patient can be made only to despair of her existence rather than to wonder in the life that has put her there. Never allow her to consider that by submitting to the Enemy's designs in their fading, she might detach herself from worldly concerns. We really cannot abide detachment in any form, and as the slow process of physical deterioration has a pesky way of reminding them of the ephemeral nature of this life and inducing in them all manner of humility by nature of their growing limitations, we must train them from an early age to regard the beauty of youth as a right rather than a gift. This allows us to elicit such anger and frustration; adult women become like children in a candy shop who, upon hearing of a limit to the number of treats they are allotted, stamp their feet, whining as they bemoan that they cannot consume the shop in its entirety — never mind that such consumption would make them sick unto death. Entitlement obscures gratitude for every gift but particularly for those gifts that are, by nature, fleeting and transient. When her daily concerns are primarily aesthetic, regarding what she sees in the mirror, she can be made to forget that all this life is but a breath, and the true reflection of her self lies inward. How easily she can be made to neglect the improvement of her soul, to bemoan the loss of lesser gifts, to despair of her own worth not reflected in the mirror, as though her visual form were all she had to offer the world. How safe a patient in this state has become from the corrupting pursuit of virtue!

Let her purchase creams and while away the hours pondering the shade of her hair or the shape of her nails. If her heart can be groomed to idolize her exterior flesh, gruesome though it may be to us, she may even fall into deep, delectable envy, the kind that manifests itself at once as seething hatred of the woman who possesses that which she lacks and of her own flesh for failing to reflect the splendor she feels is proper to her. Such a despisal of her figure is naturally nothing more than the despising of her Maker and the rejection of the form He has given her. Any time we can elicit such feelings of utter loathing in place of wretched gratitude for the gifts He has bestowed is a splendid victory for us indeed.

Of course, she may not be the sort to be taken in by excessive attendance to her appearance, in which case your only hope to stoke the fires of her vanity is to encourage her to excess rejection of attentiveness to her appearance. Women who have been taught to prize the virtue of modesty must be led to every false form of it, to eschew all forms of vanity whilst simultaneously becoming preoccupied with their renunciation of it. If your patient is among such women, she must be made to resent all implications that she ought to attend to certain so-called feminine conventions of dress or grooming. Let her think herself a lofty soul for abandoning all worldly concerns, and never let her stop to consider this as a rejection of the beauty of which the Enemy has made her the steward. From there, it is but a short leap to the interior ridicule of those women who fall on the other end of the spectrum, and you will have her marinating in the broth of her own pride in no time, leaving you to slowly increase the heat until she is boiling in self-satisfaction, all that is truly good and beautiful evaporating into thin air.

Yes, excessive vanity or total abandonment of physical beauty matters not so long as your patient can be made to steer quite clear of anything resembling that genuine modesty that She wore about herself and teaches Her daughters to emulate. Nothing like appreciation of what God has imbued her with — physically or interiorly — must enter your patient's soul. She must never be allowed to see herself as she truly is, for then she may recognize her own likeness to the Enemy and her great need of Him alike, and we cannot have her raising her arms to Him like the helpless child that she is. No, she must be led to confidence in her own powers alone, either to attain worthiness by becoming exteriorly lovely (all the while neglecting those interior qualities that are truly beautiful), or by rejecting them altogether as proof of her own spiritual superiority. As long as she believes that she reaches such heights purely by her own merits, she is safe from ever discovering the meaning of Beauty as the Enemy has intended it, and far more closely approaches the ideal of Our Father Below, who pioneered for us the example of radiating forth light by his own power, shining not in response to the Enemy, but for his own self-glorification. So long as your patient is likewise preoccupied with the endeavor of self-perfection, she is safe from the Enemy's infernal offers of purification.

With love and venom,
Boomslang

7
On Friendship

My Dear Bellbind,

I commend your recent efforts to habituate your patient firmly in the furrows of envy. Such a divisive pattern of regarding the good qualities of others with suspicion and disgust rather than gratitude and humility serves our purposes well. They must never presume the good. No longer will she be in danger of admiring that which is laudable in others or seeking to emulate their wretched patterns of behavior. In time, the contrast between her own failings and the bright sweetness of others in patience and piety will smart, the glare becoming unbearable for one whose gaze is set fixedly into shadow.

It matters not whether she *truly* falls short or does so merely from her own point of view, and in fact, our ends may be more easily accomplished if you lead the patient to ruinous dissatisfaction with her own imperfections. If left to fester, this habitual tearing apart of her own character will seep outward to poison all it touches.

And while envy is effective as broadly as it may be applied, it is perhaps nowhere more venomous than within the context of female friendships, where it can swiftly and adeptly asphyxiate those most treacherous lifelines to the Enemy.

Is there anything so wretched in the Enemy's designs as friendship? Thankfully, we have been busy redefining the concept to be an entirely self-serving endeavor. If the Enemy had His way, souls would find solace and solidarity, cheer and challenge. The fostering of faithful friendship is to be prevented at all costs via any manner of temptation. Do you realize what is at stake here? The Abomination Himself promised to be present where two or more of them gather in His name! Say what you like about the fool, He is true to his word (though His idiot insistency on honesty plays out in our favor, as the bumbling buffoon makes no attempt to hide His hand, allowing us to form our battle plans with his on full display). As iron sharpens iron, so too do the Enemy's most devoted of followers encourage and improve on one another in the most sickening displays of affection. These friendships present a grave danger to your patient, as even the most depraved of souls, if held tenderly in Christian friendship, may be raised up to the Enemy in that putrid practice we call prayer, and, though the intricacies of it remain quite obscure to us, the evidence is clear: Such prayers have sealed the fate of many a soul we thought to be entirely enmeshed in the enclave of Our Father Below. As delicious as the devouring of a soul by the slow sucking of its vitality may be to our palettes, we must bear in mind the limits of our power if we are to act effectively. This means that however close to entirely drained a patient may become, there is danger to her every second while she still lives and, more perilous still, if she is possessed of faithful friendships (a danger that continues even after death, if only these friends remember to utter the most pitiful prayer on her behalf). Be on alert! If the allies of the Enemy do not cease to lift her up to His care, there can be no rest for us; that is how certainly she will slip through our grasp with but a turn of her heart to His graces.

Still, such fetid attempts to recapture the patient from the court of Our Father Below will falter and fail absent her cooperation. The Enemy's ridiculous notions of free will are His Achilles' heel. (One really has to wonder how so powerful a being could possibly be so naive.) This is why we make it standard practice to stir up envy at every opportunity. When the rigid scales of envy properly encase her heart, every hand outreached will be met with resentment of the offeror's perceived pity and all kindness become occasion for the further hardening of her heart. When the patient sees others primarily as competition, whose success precludes her own and whose failures provide proof of her own worth, she will be shielded from love and generosity and any true communion with the other — and by proxy, from her Maker — by walls of her own making.

The object of envy is broadly irrelevant; its potency is such that any contact, no matter how miniscule, results in a pervasive poisoning of the patient. Still, it pays to be a diligent student of your patient, as that which has the greatest and most instantaneous toxicity is relative to the particulars of the individual. Is she enchanted by aesthetics, drawn in by the artifices of homemaking? Lead her away from anything resembling genuine hospitality by pricking her awareness that a friend has outdone her in creating a cozy and inviting atmosphere. Teach her to harp and nitpick on the efforts and lifestyle of the other woman, to denounce how she spends her time and money, and to discount any genuine joy that woman may find in her pursuits. You may even get a martyr out of the deal if your patient can be made to dwell on the comparative load placed upon her that prevents her from executing equally delightful decor or to despair the lack of funds that are obviously essential in creating a setting in which anyone would want to spend any meaningful amount of time.

Or perhaps your patient is an achievement-oriented woman, already primed by our prevarication of perfectionism. I must admit that this has been one of our most profitable inventions to date, and there is no shame in employing and exploiting tried-and-true methods. All that matters is where she ends up. The road by which you get her there is, in the end, irrelevant, so long as she arrives. It matters not whether she takes the swift and blazing road or if she smolders along the steep and winding path — whichever more effectively blinds and deafens her to the wiles of the Enemy.

If she is prone to perfectionism, she may be quite quick to quell overt envy. Should that be the case, you will need to be more subtle in your approach. Patients of this kind are sensitive to the injustice in their critiques of others, but that is immaterial, as they are absolute gluttons for punishing themselves. Any success of a friend is an immediate pang in her heart, a reminder of her own insufficiencies. Again, the particular achievement matters not — and this is a balm to us, as there is nearly always something to celebrate in life. A friend loses the baby weight where your patient still carries it, another receives a promotion at work while your patient wastes away repeating thankless tasks in her home, and still a third manages to homeschool her many children while your patient struggles simply to get hers in the car for school every morning. This is where exploiting their fear of vulnerability comes especially in handy: if none ever lets the others know that she is in fact a human, bearing the burdens of wrestling with her own particular circumstances, and shares only that which might prove her efforts fruitful and existence worthwhile, they become impediments to one another. No longer are they danger to us, iron sharpening iron, nor even the soft solace of mercy or empathy, but stumbling blocks, brittle burdens striking until they shatter.

Impress upon her a sense of scarcity with unceasing urgency. Once she fears that any additional light dims her own, she will dread rather than encourage any good she recognizes in others, rendering her own effectiveness in friendship utterly dull. She must remain blind to the beauty of every bloom that opens its petals to the heavens and deny the sweetness in their diversity of fragrances. She can admit no delight in that of others when their fragrance threatens to overpower hers, their beauty to leave hers unseen. Her world can admit only one permeating perfume: her own.

This is not to say that all friendships are an impediment to us. You must be discerning as you go about your business, taking care to sabotage Christian bonds of virtue while encouraging shallow, petty, and competitive relationships that bear the semblance of friendship but with none of its treacherous substance. By these pale imitations, we can erode your patient's every good tendency whilst exacerbating some of the flightier female flaws that render them innocuous to the Enemy's plans. In either case, you do well to encourage every manner of gossip, so potent a poison that only the smallest amounts are necessary to destroy entire networks of the Enemy's friends.

As to those who are not in friendship with the Enemy: It is imperative that you convince your patients of the rightness of avoiding their society (unless, of course, you think your patient likely to be drawn in by their paganism or otherwise easily susceptible to their corrupting influence). From what I can gather of your patient, it seems prudent to take steps to avoid *her* corrupting influence of those we already count among our flock. She must be made to neglect her duty to these souls, lest by proximity to her joy and kindness they be drawn from our ranks and into the fold of the Enemy. If you have been diligent about your work eliciting pride in her soul globally, it ought to be an easy enough task to draw it out here.

Perhaps the most glorious wall that can be erected against friendship is the impenetrable barrier of unforgiveness. You must seize upon every perceived slight and failure of her companions and whisper that each is directed toward her personally. She must be made to exaggerate these slights, and to smart every time she thinks of them. In time, each relationship will become no more than a cluster of wrongs, a constellation of reasons to distance herself from those who pose serious threat to our aims.

This is even more effective when the wound is deep, more substantial than a slight that is merely perceived and made to be seen as more significant than it is (although the hypocrisy we are able to elicit when a patient is on the *other* side of the argument, defending her actions to the wounded party as inconsequential in comparison with the offense taken, is truly exhilarating). Deep wounds have the potential not only to sever the nauseating bond of faithful friendship, which would be cause enough for rejoicing, but also to hollow out your patient, leaving her dry and brittle as a lifeless tree, ripe only to become the dwelling place of various insects who continue to devour it from the inside out, until nothing is left but fodder for worms and lowest of life forms that crawl the earth. Yes, she will rot, and as she does, we will make our home in the debris until nothing that bears resemblance to Him remains.

Such a result would represent an uncommonly marvelous victory for our side, and such a victory requires meticulous planning and sedulous strategy. The crucial thing with a wound of this degree is to never allow it to heal. The soul, you see, follows the manner of the body in that given time, it heals. Naturally, a certain amount of wound licking is understandable and to be expected. This is the stage to be vigilant for. You must teach your patient to continually reopen that wound, to make the wound the most significant thing about the friendship. To become susceptible to the toxic effects of unforgiveness, your patient must learn to prize her pain above her own healing. If you can produce a hardened heart that adamantly refuses forgiveness, you will have induced a self-poisoning state of the soul. Like an abscess that eventually causes sepsis, infecting the blood and destroying the body, unforgiveness eats away at every facet of a patient's virtue and psyche, dissolving it like acid. The wounding of others as she lashes out in wrath — even the complete severing of relationships — are simply added bonuses. Unforgiveness cannot destroy anyone so completely as the soul who harbors it. If you can elicit a refusal to forgive, the patient will live out her days in a prison of her own making. Though she still lives, she is as good as ensconced in Our Father's House. If you lead her down this road, she will isolate herself brick by brick, every ill wish chaining her to the desolate misery of isolation, wrath, and despair.

With love and venom,
Boomslang

8
On the Mass

My Dear Bellbind,

What pleasant news, and how fortunate, that your patient has begun to despair of her weekly visits to the Enemy's house and to eschew entirely anything beyond His basic requirements. While it is commendable to encourage self-rebuke on this matter, take care not to allow it to penetrate too deeply, lest it develop into *actual* repentance. We want her despairing of her wretchedness but never making an actual attempt to change.

Now is the time to double your efforts. When her children whine, feed her exasperation. When they squabble — *as all children do* — fix her eyes on families whose children are, for the moment, behaving as sickeningly sweet as those nauseating angels (we may as well profit something from their fleeting moment of pitiful piety and reprehensible obedience). Much safer that she should spend that hour dwelling on her own failings than to ever raise her consciousness to the Enemy or the banquet He spreads before them.

What an utter fool He is, to lay bare His dazzling brightness under the guise of such putrid material filth. And to think, He allows them to consume Him! Him, who created the universe! How He can deign to clothe Himself in the lowliest order? Why it simply reeks of weakness! He is besotted with His idiot creatures, casting His pearls before swine so blind they recognize nothing of the miracle He continually squanders on their pitiful pretense of "worship."

Our Father Below is vindicated in His rebellion by every instance of the Enemy's splendor shown forth in this universe, most abominably in the distributing of Himself to them at table. Of course, we need not witness that Abomination to see His carelessness. Just look at how liberally He sows His glory, how sloppily He spreads His own effulgence, wiping the sky even in darkness so all His world glistens. How naively He shares Himself, for if He is written into their sky, into the buzzing of their bees and the delicate beat of the hummingbird's wing, what need have they of Him? What lack of sophistication He betrays in His misplaced efforts to gather them to Himself by abandoning total transcendence for such revolting immanence. How much more totally would He captivate them if, rather than slathering their reality with Himself, He withheld all His glorious splendor as its sole possessor. What a grave and fatal error He has made not to have remained the single resplendent phenomenon of the universe. Thankfully for us, the world is alight with His fingerprints, shining palely if at all, but enough to fix their eyes to go no further.

And so it must be for your patient in the Enemy's house. If you cannot entirely distract her with the trivialities of liturgical bumbles and the irritations of her fellow man, nor to complete inattention, make her think she is there for nothing more than a therapeutic experience of self-improvement. She may indeed fall into some of the lesser virtues, but only by mere degrees. We will erode those without lifting a finger (not that we have any).

In any event, there may be no need. If you cannot keep her distracted and dejected by the "abominable" behavior of her merely average children, if she cannot be dissuaded from her habit of attendance by drawing her into the depths of discouragement, then you must wrap her up in the trivialities of the ritual. On the off chance her children adopt the occasional angelic countenance, teach her to chalk up their goodness to her own credit, and — if you can — to enjoy a self-congratulatory smirk or even self-righteous outrage at the misbehaviors of those poor pitiful other mothers whose miscreants behave as animals before their King. If, by fearsome threat or fabulous bribe, she manages to wheedle laudable behavior from her babes, use it to sate her desire for approval. You may yet turn this habit to your advantage if you can tether her mind to a weekly shot to her ego revolving around the opportunity to show off her children and family in their dress and behavior.

It matters little whether we lead her to glory in her accomplishments or despair of her failures. Both are sins of pride, blinding her to the purpose of bringing herself and her children to the renewal of His galling Covenant.

With love and venom,

Boomslang

9
On Motherhood

My Dear Bellbind,

I hear your distress that your patient's motherhood is continually causing her to run to the Enemy for assistance. You have my sympathies. It is an unfortunate feature of the Enemy's design that this particular state in life both forces them to their limits and enchants them with the Enemy's architecture, sending them running to their Maker with pleas for help and pitiful praise. Neither condition provides easy fodder for our purposes.

But do not fret. Have confidence in the ground we have laid. You must not underestimate the great ally we have in the propaganda of their culture at large. We have labored ceaselessly to produce the conditions that we now see coming to fruition. It has been a long road to twist their understanding of motherhood and new life, to eradicate the putrid stench of purity and replace it with the sultry scent of sex. We have carefully perverted their sense that the physical body carries any significance. They no longer recognize the unique role He has written into each soul, not in interior sensibility nor in material reality. They now hold that nothing exists that is outside of the material world while insisting that their flesh must be mutilated to express the idol of the immaterial self. We have engendered a confusion the depth of which is so great that, in her country at least, the typical mind holds irreconcilable opposites as gospel truth! Muddle everything. Clarity is far too stark for our purposes. We must always work in shadow.

We are nearing completion of the mission Our Father Below began long ago, when, recognizing the threat the Abomination posed in subverting the order of the universe by taking on flesh via That Woman, he determined to flout her Queenship. Queenship! What absurdity to think that a mere woman, so polluted as they all are by material flesh, could ever think to reign over purely spiritual beings! Our higher nature demands Her subservience, whatever perverted plots the Enemy has put into play. Our Father Below would not stand for this reversal of authority and labored unceasingly to undermine That Woman and all who would follow in her footsteps.

And we are nearly to the culmination of his centuries-long plan. All the signs point to it. Where the humans used to shroud their women in modesty out of respect for the feminine mystery, they now call for near-nudity of dress, echoing Our Father's cry for freedom from such arbitrary limits. They are as disgusted as we are with purity and prudence, recognizing motherhood for the true horror it is: a prison enslaving them in the chains of new children, parasites who consume all that would otherwise contribute to their mother's true glory. They are finally coming to recognize these bastards of the Enemy as the fleshy leeches they are, stealing their vitality, draining their finances, depleting their energy, robbing them of their beauty, consuming their time and their resources, swindling them of all that ought to lead to their own glory. The Enemy has the audacity to insist that they gain more than they lose, that the very act of emptying themselves *fills them up*. Stinking humility and vile subservience. He dangles for them the rotten carrot of *meaning*, and they forget all that they could become in pursuit of it. This is how He convinces them to abandon their potential for the role of automatons, pumping out hordes of Enemy slaves like factory workers on an assembly line of putrescence. Those whose minds have been liberated from His absurd propaganda have become willing disciples of Our Father Below, willing to snuff out the lives of their progeny at the outset, before they take their first breath or utter an ear-splitting cry of life.

Even those who stubbornly adhere to the Enemy's irrational stipulations are ripe in this enlightened age to see motherhood for the trap that it is, to demean and resent it as is proper. We have coached this age far from the worship of the Enemy and into the rightful worship of themselves. No longer do they imitate Him as Creator. No, they value leisure and ease over the base role of the laborer. And yet even these souls can be spun into a frenzy of activity, predicated on the inalienable values of productivity over relationship, accolades over service, acquisition over generosity, admiration over love, and achievement over dependence.

We dupe them into a lopsided view of the sexes (even as they deny their very existence!). We teach women to despise the very qualities the Enemy imbues in the feminine soul, and to prize and pursue the masculine gifts, which in turn paralyzes the masculine spirit. Having no feminine counterpart to rouse him to the heights of masculine greatness, he reverts into an eternal boyhood and can even be led to prey on those he is made to protect, to turn his strength into domination, and to victimize all who dare defy him. This is the hope of Our Father Below, in training the Enemy's slaves to do always what they wish, thus shackling themselves to their own passions and whims — willing slaves utterly unable to act as the Enemy dictates.

Of course, there is always the possibility that the Enemy's plan for motherhood has been imprinted too deeply on your patient's psyche for us to effectively corrupt it in the ideal sense. Not to worry; wherever we lack the power to divert them from the Enemy's original intentions, we need simply rely on our ability to pervert it in practice.

If you cannot make her see how vile her motherhood is, then you must train her to idolize it. Impress upon her with visions of the divine status of motherhood, all the while using images to narrow her understanding of it to a particular aesthetic. Let it not be for her an outpouring of love and generosity, nor any sort of act done in imitation of That Woman, the Abomination, or the Enemy Himself. It must become about painting a picture of lifestyle more than ever actually living one. Prompt her to lord her way of mothering over that of other women, to make *her* way, *the* way. This will be easier than you think; just look at the hatred we have managed to incite in the "mommy wars."

We have successfully taught them to relativize all that is absolute and to absolutize all that the Enemy has made genuinely subjective. The Enemy calls all mothers to bear, cherish, and will the good of their children and yet He asks many of them to do so in ways that are quite unique and would be ill-suited for the woman who has been called otherwise. We can seize upon this opportunity to sow discord among them, further dividing them and crippling them for the task of supporting or encouraging one another in fulfilling the Enemy's will. We must keep each camp about the business of insisting that its own way is paramount. While they remain engrossed in such isolating insistence on their own moral rightness, there is no threat of solidarity or community, no passing on of generational wisdom.

Those who will not be wooed by the power of independence need only be lured into self-righteousness regarding their own choices, so that they may glare haughtily at those who stray from the Enemy's teachings, all the while congratulating themselves on their great superiority, supposed purity, and freedom from error. So long as they perceive our converts as their real enemy, these supposed "disciples" will rejoice in the misery of these errant sheep, never recognizing the Enemy's deep desire to retrieve and receive His wayward flock. Those whom He asks them to pursue, they will merely condemn. Whether they know His voice or remain deaf to it is of no import whatsoever; so long as they do not act in any way that draws them closer to Him, we are victorious.

Nuance must be avoided at all costs! Turn their heads to truth *or* to compassion but be certain never to let a passion for both burn within the same soul. Only those possessed of both stand a chance of wriggling free of the clutches of Our Father Below.

With love and venom,
Boomslang

10
On Pregnancy

My Dear Bellbind,

My condolences on your patient's recent conception. The delight and the glee with which they celebrate is sickening enough, never mind the consequences. Every instance of the Enemy's Image come to bear should be at once abhorred and disavowed. You are quite right to apprehend the many dangers this pregnancy poses to your patient and the jeopardy in which our plans now hang.

All is not lost, however, as women must intentionally submit to the purifying aspects of motherhood in order for them to pose a threat. Many of them hold a falsely rosy image of motherhood, such that they are ill prepared for the heat of the Enemy's refining fire as it burns in this particular endeavor. We have just as much chance here as anywhere of corrupting His influence and impeding His plans to conform them to Himself.

You mustn't suppose that *more* children will necessarily make them holy merely by virtue of their number. They are not *more* motherly merely by the fact of more children (and in fact, mothers of more may be more easily lured into pride or overwhelm by the mere fact of their little insects increasing in numbers). No, motherhood is not a spectrum of degrees; it is an all-or-nothing state that begins at the moment a new disgusting creature claws its way into her womb. Mothers of one or many can be led as easily as single women to willingly surrender to the clutches of Our Father Below.

In some sense, this occasion should be considered a prime opportunity, for there is even *more* to exploit in her. Make her cruel to her children and despairing of herself. Never let her rash behavior raise her consciousness to her need for her Maker to supply the deficiency but let her suppose all voids are what she must herself fill, and to despair her inability to do so. They are quite inept at the project of loving when they extend no invitation to the Enemy.

Seize upon her moodiness and impress upon her how very *tired* she is. She should be made to excuse herself from as many duties as possible while balking at her husband's every offer of assistance. If you play your part well, you will have her insisting that she can do everything herself while denying that she ought to do anything at all. And the less that she does, the more easily she will fall into a miserable melancholy that will obliterate any sense of wonder or gratitude that the Enemy has seen fit to work His will of new life in her, has deigned even to touch her in the flesh, to imbue His image on the new immortal soul he has placed inside of her. *Make her forget this!*

Instead, she must be preoccupied with her own comfort at every stage. Tether her mind to thoughts of sagging breasts and hips that jiggle as they widen. Let her despair of her aching back and the weight of her exhaustion. Never let her contemplate the monumental work she does in building a new creature as the end for which she sacrifices; only allow her to despair of her condition as she would a cruel punishment and long to be relieved of it.

You might try encouraging her to devour materials about all that could go south. Even if there is no medical cause for concern, we do well to make her worry that there might be. Fan every small detail into a whirlwind of anxiety. It must be the kind of anxiety that turns her in on herself so as to keep her from seeking solace in the Enemy or worse: surrendering to Him in trust. Wherever a *fiat* is uttered in imitation of Her, a thousand agonies rip through Our Father Below and ripple through us as his henchmen. That occasion for grace alone is enough for us to fear it.

Go directly to Our Father Below and see if we cannot put an end to this nonsense before it really gathers steam.

With love and venom,
Boomslang

11
On Fertility

My Dear Bellbind,

Though in the grand scheme, your patient's miscarriage is cause for celebration, I would urge extreme caution against rejoicing just yet. You know as well as I that we could not have aborted the pregnancy unless the Enemy has permitted it, and even our greatest victories, He somehow manages to turn to His own advantage.

Remain on guard. Now is a treacherous time when suffering may actually lead your patient to cling more closely to the Enemy. These foolish, trusting sheep. Even when the evidence of His ineptitude is laid bare before them, and in the most cutting of ways imaginable, they persist in following after. She will no doubt raise her mind to Him, whether in seeking solace or as a curse. Do not think her expression of anger at Him a victory for us; *any* contact with the Enemy may be turned to His purposes and must be discouraged at every turn.

Do not think of gloating at such a time; anguish may be short-lived if, rather than despair, it paves way to deeper trust in the Enemy. Fertile or infertile, women engaging the project of welcoming new life are in the precarious position of becoming tragically aware of their true dependence on the Enemy in all things. If you cannot distract your patient, she will fall into a habit of resting in Him, of making His will her own. She cannot be allowed to surrender control, nor, in point of fact, to realize how little of it she really has. We must follow in Our Father's footsteps here: Make her think she knows best. Make her feel entirely entitled to control over her own fate so that she rejects surrender with suspicion. Present before her mind all the potential outcomes and see in them not the good that the Enemy may work, but possibilities to be regarded with fear and despair. Your patient must forget that the Enemy has promised her a future full of hope and regard the only good outcome the one she clings to as her preferred reality. Drill it into her mind: *She* knows what is best for her, and her only path to happiness is the one she imagines. She must think herself both the sailboat and the wind, one who journeys by her own power. You can never have her adapting her sails to whichever heading the Enemy might blow, else she will be in danger of actually going somewhere. No, we want her listless and stagnant, adrift in an open sea of possibilities, but unable to harness the power to move elsewhere.

The potential of this moment must be exploited. As repulsive a force as fertility may be in the production of new fleshlings, the opportunities it presents for a skilled tempter are undeniable. Women predisposed to motherly habits can be tempted to despair over the Enemy's perceived abandonment by the lack of it, while others are easily enticed to contraception by the constant impression of the great burden each new life poses to their current comforts. So pervasive is this pesticide that they have come to view their default fertility as switched "off" (as we so desperately wish it to be!) and rightly regard each new life a pest who has broken through their rightful barriers. They forget the Enemy's promise that whoever receives one child such as this receives the Enemy Himself, and thank his poor design for their short memories. Even the most faithful and fruitful of women are vulnerable to resentment of the Enemy's will when they can be led to abandon faith in His plans and taught to view their fruitfulness as a burden imposed by an overly demanding tyrant.

And while these are veritably priceless opportunities to lead our patients astray, we must never make the mistake of forgetting that these are the primary means by which the Enemy increases His foul presence in the world. He seduces them with the notion that their imperfect and faulty affection for their young mirrors His desire for them. What nonsense! He is complete, a self-sustaining, most foul exchange of persons in that most ridiculous notion of His: love. What need has He of them? And yet, they believe it, and He seems to take a perverse kind of pleasure in drawing these extraneous and unnecessary imitations of Him into His divine life. Why admit such flawed and filthy creatures? What a waste of His power, to offer them a share in His divine life. He is to be pitied if not despised for His misguided attempts to integrate these wretched creatures into what will always remain beyond their grasp. What a mercy that we have Our Father Below to show us the way, that we may not be duped as the pitiable Seraphim, condemned to a life of eternal song in praise of those infinitely more lowly than themselves.

With love and venom,
Boomslang

12
On Household Tasks

My Dear Bellbind,

Be grateful that the patient continues in her numb state. While it is not the delectable despair that we might prefer, we can be relieved that she has shown no signs of spiritual progression toward the Enemy. Now is the time to chip away at your patient's resolve to execute her duties with joy by teaching her to despise and overestimate the work involved in her vocation. You must therefore turn your attention to the patient's home life, central to the identity of all women. Can she be made to neglect her tasks while of the mind that they are both overly burdensome and beneath her?

When she sees the dishes piling up or the laundry basket overflowing, exaggerate the great burden this represents and coax every fleeting feeling of dread until they loom large in her imagination. If she dwells on a grossly exaggerated picture of the mountain of work that awaits her, she can be made to procrastinate attending to this work until the tasks feel insurmountable. This is never really the case, but if we can keep her from apprehending that fact for what it is, the menial and thankless tasks will, in her mind, begin to blot out the real significance of what she does.

So long as we can keep her mind off that, she is safe from ever offering anything for the purposes of the Enemy. We know that even the smallest task, offered in love on a whim of generosity toward her family, or — Hell forbid — a sacrifice to be joined to the suffering of the Abomination, carries within it the potential to refashion her soul to become that much more closely configured to the Enemy. This is why we make every endeavor to stir up a delicious state of resentment in our female patients, teaching them to look outward at what everyone else is failing to do (while simultaneously keeping them blind to any gratitude they may owe to others). For this technique to reach its full potency, the patient must be made to feel she is quite alone in her efforts in caring for house and home. Though this is rarely, if ever, the case, we have been so successful that it is an attitude that is nearly universal among the female sex. The righteous indignation of underappreciation is almost synonymous with motherhood, such that they even think it funny enough to jest at. It is that grain of truth massaged into the story that we tell that makes our propaganda all the more palatable to the mind that accepts it without question. Complete fabrications make our pills that much more difficult to swallow. That is why you are to dose them with just enough reality to flavor the fabrication. Unless they develop a discerning taste for the truth, a tiny measure is all you need include and they will willingly swallow a world of lies.

A pervasive sense of overwork compounded with an inflated sense of the enormity of her tasks will ideally produce one of two effects. If she is more susceptible to the soft slums of sloth, whisper devious excuses to encourage her laziness and entice her into shirking her duties. Tell her that if *she* does not mind her cluttered floor or scrambling to find a single pair of socks, why, then no one in her household should have the right to mind either. After all, she is the one doing all of the work around here! A patient cut from this cloth can become quite entitled to her lack of effort, all the while perceiving herself as the most diligent of household slaves.

Other patients are quite temperamentally unsuited for the life of a slob. They can never be contented in being overcome by clutter. Should your patient be more of this mindset, you must instead play to her anxious tendencies. Work her into a frenzy over every spot and crumb. These must become for her evidence not of the vivacity of the lives lived under her roof or the satisfaction of nourishing meals joyfully received but instead marks of both her failure and the utter indifference of her loved ones to her efforts. If they truly appreciated her, then they would not so predictably muss her meticulously arranged *mise en scène.* For that is what it is: a scene arranged for the playing out of parts, each family member not a living and breathing creature unfolding in his particularities, but a role designed to bolster the patient's self-concept by playing his part to a tee, never departing from the script that, though it stifles husband and child alike, glorifies the mother in the image to which she has become accustomed. A patient of this sort will find the daily deviations of these individuals from her ideals of them unbearable burdens. To accommodate her, the family will begin to retreat into the roles she has set for them to play, stifling all reflection of their true personality until they forget to be anything other than actors on their flawlessly prearranged stage. She will work herself to the bone and become a terror to her family, whose natural imperfections threaten the facade of perfection to which she has willingly become enslaved.

Either of these extremes will suit nicely; it matters not a wink to us whether she falls to one end or the other. What absolutely *must* be avoided is any instance of her developing *patience* for her littleness, which is symptomatic of a kind of humility that is utterly toxic to our ends. Such a posture almost inevitably leads a patient to turn to the Enemy and, though we cannot fathom what He utters to them, we see the detrimental effects of His interference in these matters. If she cannot be made to resent her work or to despair of her own insufficiency, she might attempt to offer her minuscule and even incomplete efforts to the Enemy. And He has the audacity to accept! Should she attempt this, we may as well abandon our efforts on this front entirely, for the battle has been lost. All the intelligence we have gathered from past skirmishes tells us that not only will the Enemy accept such pitiful substitutes in place of a job well done but that He Himself will supply the difference! How He manages to maintain the upper hand while rewarding such substandard achievement boggles the mind.

We are forced to relive the horror of the loaves and fishes all over again; such an insurmountable attack to lay them under the siege of hunger during the most pivotal of the Abomination's nasty talks and with one simple act of absurdly deficient generosity we are entirely undone! However naive the Enemy may appear or however vulgar in His infatuation with His creatures, you must never underestimate His cunning. The infernal truth of it is that He *can* supply for your patient's deficiencies, and He *will* make up for what she lacks, if only presented with the invitation. *You must keep her from turning mind and heart toward Him!* Do you not by now recognize how costly that is? How, at any moment, all our efforts might be entirely overturned by one simple glance at the Enemy? Whatever the case, you must silence her. The Enemy will not advance in lieu of her invitation, but a single word from her and we may find all ground we have gained lost in an instant.

With love and venom,
Boomslang

13
On Children

My Dear Bellbind,

You seem to be making adequate progress on your patient's resentment of her daily tasks. I urge you not to be too self-congratulatory. Do not let up your efforts. In fact, you must double them. And yet, you must take care not to concentrate all those efforts in a single area, lest she become wise to your attentions.

You have sown the seeds of resentment in the fields of her basic household tasks. Now, you are ready to reap your rewards. True as it may be that any deterrence from her vocation faithfully lived is an accomplishment worthy of celebration on our part, we have only just begun to lay the ground for the work we wish to do in her soul. Think of it as a house if you'd like; we have laid the foundation, but we have much to do before we are ready to settle in and make ourselves at home.

The time is ripe when habitual resentment begins to seep into all aspects of your patient's life and, in particular, into her interactions with her children. Some degree of annoyance is merely natural among souls who spend any significant amount of time together. Our aim, then, is to prey upon this natural vulnerability until she comes not only to accept this reality but to answer willingly when the habit beckons. Teach her to regard every irksome behavior not as a natural result typical of a development stage but as an intolerable vexation that must be stamped out. The child, you see, will have no concept of how bothersome his behavior is. What he needs to overcome his innate childishness is patience and explanation. If your patient can be led to respond with disdain when he persists, every little irksome trait can become a trigger for her to fly off the handle. This is quite confusing for the child, who will either delight in the attention he has managed to garner with little effort or else go to pieces in a tantrum that will itself be trying to the mother as it overloads her nervous system.

We must make every effort to exploit these physical vulnerabilities, as the hormonal impulse to nurture her children is a formidable barrier we must overcome and habituate her away from. When properly executed, our plan of attack will negate the nurturing effects of her hormones, turning her inward and away from any act of patience or generosity toward her children. In time, she will come to regard the helplessness of her children with impatience and disgust, thinking only of the imposition to herself and everything she would rather be doing. This is best accomplished in moments of interruption, and your attentiveness in these moments will be critical.

Interruptions are generally moments when the Enemy tries to pull our patients outside of themselves, redirecting their attentiveness to some project of His own or some quality He wishes to strengthen in them. If you stroke your patient's ego just right, she can be made to regard uninterrupted projects as her right, a domain free from impingement in which she rules as sovereign queen. Under this entirely laughable framework, any interruption becomes a grave violation of her authority and due justice. Thus, rage rather than restraint becomes her rote response.

Naturally, this is a delightful inversion of what the Enemy wishes for His subjects. His primary directive for her at any moment is to respond to her children's needs with patience, to sacrifice her own wants, needs, and desires for their sake. If your patient is particularly prone to this posture, you need only lean into this tendency until she forgets herself entirely and fails to honor His commands to attend to her own needs, which will render her utterly unable to care for anyone at all. But if your patient has become enamored of the illusion of her authority in the household arising primarily from the respect and deference shown to her, rather than the posture of service espoused by the Enemy, you have the great hope of making her a tyrant yet.

Patience is to be avoided, whatever the cost. If your

patient's children are met with patience, they might get the idea that they are lovable creatures, entirely worthwhile — as shown by the example of your patient's time and attention. I know that the brats are not *your* patients, but is the world not more tolerable the fewer souls believe themselves worthy of love and affection?

Oh, sickening affection! Do your best to prevent your patient from such vulgar displays. They are all too likely to be the spark that ignites the wildfire of self-sacrificial love, in which all our efforts may be rapidly consumed, until nothing of us remains in her. Annoyance and affection are diametrically opposed; take care to expand the one and you will snuff out the other. Never let her pause to consider her own role in her children's behavior, whether it might result from hunger or lack of sleep or overscheduling. No, she must reflexively and unconsciously view every irritation as an intentional misbehavior, evidence of her parental failures and the unacceptability of the child before her.

Leaving her time for reflection on the cause of the annoying behavior may result in empathy or compassion and is all too likely to lead to patience and consideration. If this occurs, not only is our opportunity lost, it has become occasion for the growth of virtue, that invasive weed, which must be ripped out at its roots before it renders the soil of her soul toxic to the seeds we have so diligently sown.

If you can lead her to ruminate on her children's flaws in their absence, so much the better. Let her gripe and bemoan their faults and failings in the presence of other mothers, so that they, too, might become inured to these infectious attitudes. In point of fact, this is much more easily accomplished with husbands (more on that when next I write), as disdain for her children, even if properly fostered within her innermost thoughts, remains contrary to a mother's social programming. At best, you might hope to lure her into humorous jabs about her children as "little monsters" or "noisy animals" — anything that at first appears harmless, but when habitually repeated in chorus undermines her operative concept of their value and dignity. There is no harm in her maintaining a mental assent to her children's worth, so long as she can be made to treat them otherwise. Let her speak of them with scorn and laugh, all the while insisting that she treasures them dearly. So much the better, as women of this sort are unlikely to become wise to just how closely, in word and deed, they mimic our own disdain for the lamentable little fleshlings.

With love and venom,
Boomslang

14
On the Husband

My Dear Bellbind,

Do not take your patient's persistent love for her children as a sign of defeat. There is much more we can work in a soul such as this. We need simply turn her affection for them to our advantage, for virtue can only remain a danger to us if it cannot be taken to extremes.

You must shift the battleground. Whenever opportunity presents itself, continue to erode her affection and undermine her dedication to her children. This is always desirable. But a change of tactic may be in order if your patient is more susceptible to resentment of her husband. If so, you are in luck: resentment of a spouse is much more easily cultivated than resentment of children!

We have a veritably endless trove of tactics at our disposal to destroy spousal love, and so much the better.

The Enemy has seen fit to create marriage as a reflection of His own communal nature; thus it must be the central thrust of our attack. We cannot have His ideals reflected clearly into the world. We must distort and twist them, so that the original attraction remains intact, but the execution leads them further from His designs for them. We have made great headway via our messaging on marriage as the gateway to personal fulfillment and in leading spouses to destroy each other, the institution of the supposed love, and the security their offspring find therein.

Each spouse tells himself or herself (at our direction) that his or her own personal happiness is the height of the good he or she ought to pursue, and we show each just what an obstacle the other becomes. For, as the Enemy has designed it, the married couple ought to be engaged in mutual self-giving. They are to imitate the Abomination in self-sacrifice. This is quite naturally repugnant to those who do not fully understand the Enemy's refining purposes for the Sacrament, so our work here is rather simple. Do not be overly concerned with ripping apart what the Enemy has so perversely attempted to join. Delicious though it may be, such complete division is ultimately unnecessary. Even those who commit to a lifetime together can be led to create for themselves a hellish landscape of self-centered designs, and with very little prompting from us.

Instill in your patient a deep-seated and unconscious fear of being controlled. Whisper softly (so as to be undetected) that she must look out for her own good and that to surrender herself entirely to the good will of her husband is to make a monumental mistake. Keep her from examining this fear, for if she holds it up to his character it will wither away by comparison, an obvious illusion. Unchecked, however, this fear can become the controlling interest in your patient's behavior. The more she insists on control, the more she alienates her husband, who only desires her respect and whose own self-respect rests on the life he provides for her. As she insists on her own way, her spouse will most likely allow her to have it; men of his ilk seldom like to make waves. But over time, this lack of trust will erode their bond and even erect a barrier between them. He wishes to give, you see, and one who controls can never receive. Thus, discouraged, he surrenders to his wife's will; and she, though given all the control she insists on, is left wondering why her husband no longer bothers about wooing her in the way to which she had once grown accustomed.

Encourage all manner of griping about his habits. Humans love to speculate on any flaw, no matter how insignificant, that they recognize in the other. So much the better when we can coax them to point fingers while remaining entirely blind to the way those characteristics they so despise in others manifest in themselves. Incite gossip about her husband's failings with her girlfriends. Lead her to sacrifice *him* for the sake of shared intimacy with *them*, never realizing how deeply this undermines his standing in her heart.

When he takes leave of her, instruct her to punish him and make him pay dearly for his absence. Whether it is for work or recreation, it is no matter. Both are necessary for him and must become reflexively vile to her. If you can coordinate with his tempter to work up feelings of smothering and entrapment, so much the better. You must do what you can to lead her to infantilize and mistrust the husband at every turn. Encourage every form of small dishonesty; she must convince herself that her lies are justifiable to shield her from his tyranny. Seize upon any item left out of place or chore left undone to leave her huffing about doing all herself, taking him entirely for granted.

As for the children, let her fuss over them. Encourage it! If she makes them her all, in a constant state of sacrifice for them and never for the husband, she will grow in affection for her children and her feelings for him will become stale and liable to crack. Let her brood over them such that she forgets they are rightfully his as well, so that she comes to resent any attempt to interfere with her rule of the roost. When it becomes clear that she holds no regard for his judgments regarding their safety or basic needs and thinks him inept, he will more than likely throw up his hands in defeat and surrender the domain of the children to her entirely, at which point you can remount your attack on his character and foster further resentment for his lack of equal participation in management of the household.

Disagreements are not so much a victory for us as a fact of the institution of marriage; it is what you make of them that counts. It will be most profitable if they can be made to turn on each other. When in doubt, remember this rule of thumb: the destruction of their mutual affection is most effectively accomplished when they are led to make mountains out of molehills and molehills out of mountains. Teach her to object to the amount of time her husband devotes to his Saturday morning golf routine, assuring her that it must be a sign not of his need for recreation but of his lack of affection for her. When he offers to assist with the dishes, let his kindness ring in her ears as disapproval of her household management. Meanwhile, whisper that her engagement with late-night romance novels is trivial, meaningless, and not at all occasion for her growing discontent with her husband's lack of resemblance to the caricatures of masculinity therein. This kind of hypocrisy and insecurity form the basis of many marital dissolutions. Why, Griseo once had a similarly afflicted patient shrieking like a banshee after glancing up from her steamy novel to notice her husband's Instagram feed — never mind that the scantily clad figure on screen was, in fact, his cousin.

Now we turn to the bedroom. As the Enemy intends it to be the exemplar of His love, the zenith of all His unitive measures, it is a central battleground for our attack. Fortunately, few manage to scale their way to the heights of the glory He offers, content to graze upon the grasses of the lowest and most accessible meadows, never even offering so much as a glance at the summit. You must teach her to withhold intimacy, cheapening it to currency. When she offers her body as reward for this or that, she makes herself a token for manipulation. Never allow her to enter into the free exchange of self! So long as she enters into the marital act with the idea that it is given in exchange for some other good — even for her own pleasure — and not sought for the sake of unity itself, you will have successfully avoided the worst of dangers.

The Enemy's invention of pleasure, though absurd by its own merits, has proven quite useful to us. We need not lure them into totalizing misery if we can but engineer a restructuring of goods so that the lesser obscure the higher. Having a foretaste of what is greater cannot be a danger to us if their sight is so obscured, for they almost inevitably pursue the lesser good as its own end with no regard for what the Enemy actually wishes to give them. His plans are thwarted when the enticement of the lesser thing becomes all that their greedy little hearts seek after. The wisest tempters seek not to deprive their patients of these little pleasures but to bury them to the neck, that by their sheer weight, they may be rendered immobile, left to suffocate and starve, filled with the temporal but utterly deprived of all that truly satisfies.

Our project of lustful degradation has been so successful that few, if any, experience this exchange as anything more than a rubbing of bodies for the purpose of self-pleasure. Unity is nearly a thing of the past, and we have successfully persuaded many to share our repugnance for procreation. Even those who prize it, who cannot be made to sacrifice it as an ideal, can be made to *fear* it, and on a practical level, that is equally suitable to our ends if not our tastes.

If all else fails, make her husband the god of her worship, the singular object of her adoration. Let her seek from him what the Enemy intends to offer her in Himself. While this may result in an amicable union for a time, we are in it for the long game. She will seek from her husband satisfaction that he can never offer, and the resulting anguish will inevitably decay the bond between them. Unions of this sort offer the appearance of love with none of its freedom. And, as they are utterly inept at the project of loving — save the Enemy's grace to supply for their deficiencies — the more they seek the infinite from a finite spouse, the more they find their partner wanting. Naturally, this leads to a focus on consuming the other rather than laying down the self. And, in the end, is this not precisely Our Father's dream for his subjects?

With love and venom,
Boomslang

15
On the Mother-in-Law

My Dear Bellbind,

How delightful that your efforts are producing such friction between the spouses. We must endeavor to widen this gap until it becomes an untraversable chasm. Now that conditions are inhospitable within the home, they are in fact ideal for increasing tension with the patient's mother-in-law.

The key to fostering familial divisions is to prey on their fragile egos by teaching each woman in turn to perceive every action on the part of the other as a personal slight, no matter why it was done or how it was intended. You must create a filter through which all actions pass, so that your patient keeps a personal record of wrongs that exist largely, if not entirely, in her own mind. Every behavior of the other, every action taken, must be seen in the most uncharitable light possible. She must presume ill will at every turn.

Teach her to store up each wrong, to treat every slight as a pet over which she continually ruminates until at last she cannot contain her fury. Let her revel in passive-aggressive splendor, never being frank about her preferences and distaste but always proceeding with the air of one who is slightly displeased. Others will learn to walk on eggshells to avoid her wrath but, because of the filters you have effectively erected, even the most considerate actions will be displeasing to her for she will be well practiced at finding fault in even those choices that have nothing to do with her whatsoever.

She must seek to be the sole possessor of the unadulterated affection of her husband, regarding his approval as a kind of trophy, the attainment of which requires the utter vanquishment of her enemy. Thus, each woman will be vying for his affections while plotting the destruction of the other most dear to his heart.

Never mind that, under better circumstances, she might have had a warm and delightful friend, full of wisdom and counsel, holding her as dearly as she held her own son. That is, in fact, the kind of bond that plays right into the Enemy's hands. She must never consider what she sacrifices when she holds so tightly to her trove of imagined grievances. Teach her to grip them tightly, to refuse to let go of a single one so that, though her knuckles be raw and bleeding, the thought of letting go never crosses her mind.

Let her imagine every way to dig and jab, to return

evil for evil (or even evil for imagined evil, such as the case may be). If she will play the victim, so much the better. If she insists that every member of the extended family must know how aggrieved she is, how her husband's mother has wronged her, she will be sure to both wreak havoc on the familial bonds at large and widen the gap between reality and her own perception of it, sinking deep into the mire of her own hateful resentment.

From here, your patient can be led to withhold her children from her mother-in-law. Let her ride the wave of righteous indignation into the very palm of Our Father Below. Your patient will leap at every opportunity to remind her mother-in-law that *she* is the gatekeeper to her home, her children, and her husband and that she will wield her power to crush every small hope of connection unless her mother-in-law complies with your patient's every directive. That should stamp out any lingering goodwill her mother-in-law may carry for her son's sake and, given time, will either give rise to a great battle between the warring women or else the mother-in-law will simply slink away, nursing her wounds and grieving what has been lost.

All of the above assumes that your patient's mother-in-law is of a mind to accept your patient as a daughter of her own, in which case, the program I have described will be effective at eliminating this threat and depriving the family of a further source of maternal love and wisdom. Is her mother-in-law of a different sort? Perhaps she is a nasty and broken creature. If so, you may be more successful in keeping her around to perpetuate the infliction of generational wounds and to expose your patient's children to the type of familial dysfunction we so gleefully engender as frequently as possible. Convince your patient that to forgive means to submit to continual abuses and to teach her children to likewise become emotional punching bags for the indulgence of their grandmother's vicious will. After all, the Enemy teaches them to "turn the other cheek." Many a soul has strayed from the Enemy's camp precisely because we convince them that the abuse they have suffered is His will for them.

With love and venom,
Boomslang

16
On the Home

My Dear Bellbind,

I see now from your last letter that your patient will not be dissuaded from her tasks and, though we have heretofore chosen the wrong tack, this is easily corrected. We have no major obstacle to overcome; this new data merely indicates that we will be more successful in tempting your patient toward sloth's opposite but equally damning cousin: overwork.

This cannot be done by weighing the patient down with the *burden* of the work but rather by guising temptation in the *delight* of homemaking. So long as the patient can be encouraged in the frivolities of the house décor and appearance, the danger of "home" will become ever more elusive as she frets over this or that perceived imperfection.

We have quite the ally in the visual aids offered by

today's media. The Home and Garden Network is demolishing and renovating on demand and scores of women post videos of themselves cleaning their perfectly manicured mansions, themselves dolled up to the nines while elbow deep in toilets. Tug at her heartstrings. Let these images be to her a siren's song, emblematic of the heights of perfection she must attain as keeper of her home. Show her what it means to be a woman: the keeper of a beautiful space, the painter of a tableau of domestic tranquility.

If she can be made to fret over her appearance and that of the house, she may be led to an obsession with cleanliness and a spirit of competition with the neighbors — a well-tended garden or seasonal porch display will do nicely as a spark. See if you cannot also build upon the foundation of consumerism we have laid, encouraging her to spend her last penny and beyond, justifying her purchases as *necessary* to keep her home continually decked in the sights and sounds of the season. All the better if you can convince her to view her husband as a spendthrift tyrant from whom all her purchases must be secreted away. Thus, you will have convinced her both to break her agreements regarding spending limits with the added betrayal of deception to conceal her financial infidelity. Consume her with affairs of such little import that she may be made to abandon those tasks that have a real stake in eternity.

Such preoccupations are ripe, nay, dripping with potential for our aims. A woman such as this may suffer such scrupulosity over the stains on the couch that she will refuse to receive visitors altogether. She may even seethe with resentment at the little hands that made them and come to see such stains as evidence not of a happy home humming with life unfolding in its natural state but as the cruel punishment of Sisyphus: the constant and maddeningly dull trudging uphill under the heavy burden of her mindless and repetitive task. Those for whom she once labored to create the warmth of home become, in her mind, most lazy and ungrateful impediments to the attainment of the domestic perfection that rightly belongs to her in view of her efforts.

Remember, in this respect, it is her *attitude* that is the problem; our effect on her performance of her duties is secondary. The posture that poses the greatest danger to us is one of prayer, creativity, joy, and spontaneity. We want her stagnant, never choosing what is important over that which is urgent or pressing. We want her frantic. She must be so, if we are to foster the overwhelm and despair that will render her efforts meaningless and her home without joy.

With love and venom,
Boomslang

17
On Appearances

My Dear Bellbind,

I am encouraged to hear of your progress in encouraging the patient's vanity. If I might be so bold, I submit to you that we have found the key to this patient. Can she be tempted to excessive concern over her appearance? Indeed, there are few who cannot, and there is much delicious suffering to be gleaned if the effects of this single temptation can only seep their poison further into the patient's mind and relationships.

Once the patient despairs of her own worth and centers her critical eye on her body while becoming nearly blind and entirely indifferent to the state of her soul, you can foment envy of others' looks in her heart so that the gifts of youth and beauty become bitter stumbling blocks and preoccupy her mind in all public spaces and private meetings.

Once envy has taken root, it is a short leap for your patient to imagine her husband's affection for other women, which you can and should facilitate. Remind her of how he once looked at her, and whisper to her that he no longer sees such riches in her countenance but that every glance and gesture toward another woman is in fact rooted in his dissatisfaction with her physical deterioration. Time and childbearing have worked their magic for us on her face and curves, and we have seen to it that their perception of beauty is mutually exclusive with these hallmarks of motherhood. Let her scrutinize her husband's behavior such that the simple effects of habit and familiarity become to her the proof that he has reached a state of total disinterest in her.

You must make every effort to have your patient consume herself in the pain of her husband's imagined rejection. Clothe it in anger. In fury, let her withhold her own affection from him in response. These kinds of lover's tiffs create a feedback loop that nearly always destroys, if not both parties, their mutual affection (which is at least half as good). The effectiveness of this technique lies in the fact that it requires no actual lessening in affection but merely in staving the *flow* of affection exchanged between spouses. Many a lover has been demoted to roommate under this technique that requires minimal effort on our part (which is why we employ it so freely). You can stunt the deepening of their love and possibly even undo its maddening effects. Make her think it was never as lovely as she once thought or, better yet, entirely a figment of her imagination. Lead her into disillusionment with the ebb and flow of romance that is only natural to their material state. She must be made to think every lull a permanent crisis, entirely irreversible.

Lead her into a desperate panic. Encourage the consumption of all manner of materials — books, podcasts, magazine articles — on recapturing a husband's attentions. Allow her to put great effort into improving her *appearance* but never her actual *behavior* toward him. Ensure that she is never in danger of extending anything that stands a real shot at bridging the chasm we have opened between them. So many a marriage has fallen simply because a man fails to notice newly trimmed bangs! Rarely do they fail to notice an increase in warmth and affection, so keep her mind on that new dress. Under these conditions, she might be led to despair over the lack of response on his part, taking it as a sign that what was once there is no longer salvageable, if it was even ever real to begin with. Let her fantasize about the romance she might find with *other* men who are no more than a caricature of figures she has seen in books and television, basically lovesick slaves who bear no semblance to any man in reality. Let her fawn over the imaginary life she might have with someone so fully devoted to her, never mind that in real life someone so devoid of person would be utterly uninteresting.

One side benefit of weaving your way into her imagination in this regard is that she will begin to fear that he has strayed in the very same way. And yet while she feels a great deal of compassion for herself and feels mostly if not entirely justified in her fantasies, the very idea that he may be untrue will wound her to the core. She will make of herself a martyr, and her pain will become dearer to her than any distant memory of her husband's love. In time, you may be so successful as to stir her into jealous rages and, if you are, I commend you. But do not discount the subtle wounds of mere bitter conversation; given enough time, her bitterness toward him — warranted or not — will, in effect, drive him further from her, despite the wedge being imaginary to begin with.

Once envy and bitterness characterize the patient's most central relationship, compromising her access to deleterious effects of love, you pave the way to cultivate the patient's dissatisfaction with herself. If she can be made to ruminate on every physical flaw, she may even be susceptible to despair in dieting and laziness in her health. She can be led to misuse and abuse herself to the point of utter disdain. But more on that in my next letter. You should have enough to occupy you for the time being as you lead her to undermine her sense of self as you both narrow it to the physical realm and devalue what she finds there.

With love and venom,
Boomslang

18
On Pride

My Dear Bellbind,

From what you have told me, you realize as well as I do that now is a delicate moment. You have successfully driven your patient to despair of her husband's affections, entirely imagined and utterly unbeknownst to him. Well done!

Can you seize this opportunity to encourage her to sloth and hopelessness? Whether she believes that her physical appearance is the pinnacle of female achievement or a vanity beneath her consideration (either will do), whisper to her that it is beyond hope. Remind her that female beauty is only to be found in the impossible perfection we paint, the likes of which she will never achieve. If she can be made to believe that control is entirely outside of her grasp, any effort toward maintaining her health will appear useless, and we can stop her in her tracks.

This will, of course, mark her as a failure in her own eyes, when in fact the real failure we have produced in her lies within her unwillingness to try. If she does make an attempt, be sure that it is short lived. This is a less sure path to our ends but may be worth the extra effort in the deep despair you can elicit. Each time she falters, impress upon her the impossibility of her goals. Never mind that any small improvement in her habits offers immediate benefits to her health, nor that such gains are more proper a reception of the Enemy's gift of health; incremental improvements are never satisfactory to the vanity of fleshlings, as they so easily believe their worth lies only in reaching the pinnacle of an achievement and never in the actual effort it takes to make the climb. Thus, they see the large gap from where they begin to the place they wish to go and respond reflexively: "It is too far," and strand themselves upon the very spot where they stand. We need have no fear of their progress once they tell themselves their goal is perpetually out of reach. Then, we need only begin a project of dark whisperings of their insufficiency so that they hurl themselves into a spiral of self-reproach. Then, we have them right where we want them: despising themselves for failing to achieve what they believe they want but were unwilling to act to attain.

If she is not the sort to be tempted to inaction, you need only push her to the opposite extreme. Those given to excess of activity scarcely rest, let alone fall into sloth, but this poses no impediment to our aims. Souls of this sort are easily led to equate output with worth; they overvalue *doing* at the expense of *being* and *accomplishment* at the expense of *presence*. Make her dizzy! Make her dance. Make her go to the extreme, and all the while whisper the steady chant: *It will never be enough*. Whip up a frenetic frenzy and let her spin until she is so disoriented that rest is but a memory and any pause becomes for her an unstable state so that she must maintain her motion or topple entirely. Allow no state in between.

You may think a patient like this is a lost cause in terms of fixation on appearance, but nothing could be further from the truth. The fact that she is now eating healthily and exercising regularly can be turned to advantage by a skillful tempter. A patient of this sort, with her propensity for perfection and vanity, may yet be led off the treacherous path of self-improvement and safely into the path of self-destruction *if* she can be led to an eating disorder, the scrupulous cousin of intemperance. Make her see her imperfections via the lens of despair. She must not be allowed a clear view of herself nor compassion for her genuine limitations; that is the treacherous way of humility. No, you must lead her into a melancholic medley of pride and despair: despair of her lack of perfection and pride in believing that perfection attainable. If she can be made to withhold from her "unworthy" self the basic good of sustenance, you can be sure the damage she does to her psyche inflicts the same degree of damage to her bodily health, possibly greater.

And the delicious bit of it all is that in both instances — in sloth or overwork, in disregard for health or obsession with it — an awareness of the influence of pride will hardly cross the patient's mind! She thinks her opinion of herself so lowly that she will believe herself humble, when in reality that repellent virtue is, given her current state, almost entirely out of her reach. Souls who despise themselves and mourn their lack of perceived glory operate out of a state of deep pride. They mistakenly believe that they are the source of their own light and bemoan their incapacity to shine as brightly as they believe that they ought, nay, deserve. Had they any vision at all, they would easily perceive that all light comes from the Enemy and those who shine around them have but submitted to His notions of cleanliness, which, although we cannot perceive clearly due to that light's piercing brightness, we assume allows them to more effectively reflect His burning effulgence. The prideful souls wish to possess this brightness for themselves, to glow from within, and give no thought to how they might surrender to the Enemy's work in them. Such work is painful to them, more so when they attempt to clothe themselves in the glories of the world. Some of these earthly glories stick so effectively to mind and spirit that the separation of soul from this adhesive armor requires great force; whether it is pulled away gradually or ripped in a moment, the pain of separating what was once so intimately attached burns in the intermediate, though it may yield lightness and freedom in the long term. Even when it is shed, remnants of the adhesive are slow to rub off and leave the soul dim and unreflective for some time to come.

Our goal is nothing more than to show them every bit of armor we possess, to make it all so shiny and appealing, that, bit by bit, as they take them on, they become weighed down with the heaviness of their chosen personas. This has the effect of turning them almost to stone, rendering them both unwilling and unable to respond to the Enemy's call with the agility, speed, and flexibility that He demands. The more armor they accept and pile on, the more firmly rooted they become, immobile and unyielding idols in an ever-darkening prison of their own design. And they do so grow to love their prisons! This is what Our Father Below wishes to grant every soul who has suffered enfleshment at the hands of the Enemy. Hell is, as we well know, an eternal asylum for the rebel who refuses to bend the knee and the madman who makes himself the center of the universe.

With love and venom,
Boomslang

19
On Scripture

My Dear Bellbind,

In my earlier years, I would have chastised you soundly for the grave error you have made. In point of fact, a greener version of myself would have shrieked in fury, possibly abandoning you altogether in just punishment for the idiocy you have displayed in allowing your patient to act on her lingering impulse to pursue the Enemy's nefarious Word. Far more despicable souls have been lost to us after coming into contact with the presence He has imbued in His infernal, blithering Scriptures.

It should go without saying, but I will force myself to make plain to you what ought to be obvious as the most basic tenet of the tempter. Let me be clear, you pathetic weed: You must keep the patient away from the Enemy's Word! This is no mere book; the last smoldering embers of nearly extinguished souls have been reignited, set ablaze by the merest spark set off by its pages. There is nothing so destructive to our aims as a patient who willingly submits herself to any of the ways the Enemy makes Himself manifest in the world. To encounter His Word is to encounter the fleshy Abomination that Our Father Below has so rightfully railed against, and there is nothing so damnable as the merest hint of the Enemy's most repulsive inventions — despicable love, reprehensible mercy, salvation most foul — coming into even the most fleeting contact with the willing heart of a vulnerable patient. A patient in regular contact with the Word may shake off the chains of the Father below and treat his shackles as nothing. This, of course, will not do, as the only worthy end for these humans is to writhe in misery under Our Father's dutiful scrutiny.

If you cannot curb your patient's curiosity, flood her with commentaries. Let her substitute the revelations of another, the more errant the better. Though none is infallible, it is obviously more suitable that she pursue false interpretations and, if that is not possible, purely emotive ones. Remind her that the text of Scripture is old, obtuse, and dull. She has heard it before! Impress upon her that there is nothing new to discover and, if you cannot stir up boredom or stave curiosity, keep her focus narrow and cultivate in her a delicate taste limited to those passages that leave her feeling uplifted and encouraged. I know that these can be precarious strategies but, with a persistent case like this, our best hope is to lure her away from those conditions that might lead to contact with the Enemy and all its unpredictability (indeed, the only predictable facet of such contact is its destructive effects on our endeavors, its impediments to our aims). In other words, make her pursue the carrot and not its Maker. Teach her to love the sweetness of the Enemy without ever knowing *Him*. When she ponders that which is mysterious, let her throw up her hands. When she encounters something in the Word that contradicts with her ideas of how things ought to be, do not allow her to question her sense of what constitutes rightness but instead to object only to the Word itself, to assume that it is the Word and never she who is flawed. Run each and every passage through the filter of the god whom she has constructed in her mind, retaining that which confirms her concept of the Enemy and rejecting all that contradicts this smaller, meager image.

Never allow the Word to actually inform this image. We have a great ally in the world here, which insists on a laughable shell of compassion that boils down to permissive acceptance. We have instilled as a bedrock of the human culture the notion that challenge is incompatible with love. What we have taught them to call "love" bears little resemblance to the concept as the Enemy has conceived it. Our propaganda is effective precisely because we retain *just enough* of the Enemy's inventions while hollowing them into mere shells of their original meaning. In that void, we insert every kind of deviation and impediment to the Enemy's aims that we can reasonably harbor under the guise of His inventions. We penetrate their defenses with a Trojan horse of sorts; the appearance of a gift that contains the means of their demise.

Once we have stripped values from the bedrock of truth, we can give these words any meaning whatsoever. Divorced from their original intentions, they can be directed to invalidate any self-revelation He offers them. For when we can show them that it contradicts entirely — or indeed, just enough — with what we have taught them to hold sacrosanct, we can encourage them to reject His Word on the grounds that it violates those very concepts that we have commandeered and redefined (and they have embraced) according to our purposes. We see that our labor has not been in vain when they bend to the judge and jury of public opinion, which ebbs and flows on the shifting sands of trends and time rather than on His Word, which is the most dangerously solid ground from which they might derive their values. Thus, man no longer holds concepts up to the Word as a litmus test for their veracity and value but rather holds the Word up to our concepts and, by our designs, finds it very much wanting. *O tempora, O mores*, indeed!

With love and venom,
Boomslang

20
On Worldly Advice

My Dear Bellbind,

It is startling news to hear that the patient's children are beginning to utter prayers to the Enemy, but I suppose it ought not to be. It is par for the course with patients of this sort, I'm afraid. Particularly as we "overdo it" in certain aspects; your patient has only to turn on the news and despair the state of the world and she will be sprinting to the Enemy like the sniveling wretch she is, desperate for Him to shelter her children from the havoc we are wreaking around them.

As much as you are able, you must divert her motherly impulses away from those activities that lead toward the Enemy, channeling them — anywhere else! Lead her to a place of fear, so that she might over parent any creativity or individual impulse right out of them. As a side effect of these repressive tactics, the children of such parents are easily lured by that which has been withheld from them and made to appear tantalizing by such limits that they become easy prey for us. They will fixate on what they are deprived of so that, once the parental hold loosens even slightly, those limits will be the first place the children tread with their newfound freedom. Do your job well and you will make light work for their future tempters and reap the burdens of your patient's misery as she ruminates on her failures for decades to come.

If she will not be overbearing, then let her become too permissive. Immerse her in worldly advice to prize her children as "buddies" and, by their adoration, feed her ego. Let her always be following their lead, allowing them "choice" in everything from their own curfew to exacting their own punishment for their transgressions — even in choosing their religion. We have reaped a bountiful harvest of delectable "nones" by convincing them that any exposure to the Enemy's wiles leaves a child less free. Left to their natural inclinations, with no input from the Enemy regarding his absurd notions, they trickle into our camp quite freely, with nothing to fortify or incite resistance. They honestly believe they do their children a service by keeping them ignorant of the Enemy's rules and traditions, stunting their spiritual growth even to the point that they lack entirely the language to articulate their spiritual yearnings and appetites. Hammer in the battle cry: no narrative but their own! For as surely as a toddler will scribble nothingness and claim to write his own name, these children will wander about, lost in a fantasy of spirituality that bears no semblance whatsoever to the concrete Reality to which the Enemy beckons. Thankfully, by their negligence, parents of this sort all but deafen their children to the tones in which He calls.

And do not whine to me that the little brats are not yours to corrupt! We must all do our part to keep the smallest of souls from any danger of that wretched virtue that leads straight to intimacy with the Enemy. Their innocence is foul enough. To allow even the smallest step toward the Enemy is a grave offense. The earlier they can be enticed to our ways, the more assuredly they will remain in them, continuing safely down into the hands of Our Father Below.

With love and venom,
Boomslang

21
On the Present Moment

My Dear Bellbind,

This is indeed a heavy day and I mourn alongside you. Still, we mustn't wallow in your failures but continue on with our projects, however dim our hopes may now be. The sooner we accept the state of things, the sooner we can respond with the severe measures they require.

You must reconcile yourself to this truth: we cannot have her heart, for He has won it. She has given it away and it resides where we cannot grasp. Do not despair. While the heart is truly the sweetest victory won, we do not need her heart — as long as we manage to capture her attention. Not that we want it on consciously on *us*, by no means! The less she considers our influence, the better.

The truth of it, I'm afraid, is this: You must give up on your aim of tempting her to overt vices (for now).

She has achieved a kind of clarity and rhythm of reception of sacramental graces that will insulate her from earning a place among our masterpieces. But do not lose hope! We may still secure for her a lesser place in Our Father's chambers if we are careful to lurk undetected, biding our time with gradual and obscure temptations. Death by a thousand cuts, after all, still accomplishes its end of the extinguishment of life; in spectacular and quiet deaths alike, men breathe their last. So too it must be with her soul.

Begin by coaxing the patient to live in the past, or the future for that matter — so long as she avoids the *present* moment; it matters not that the Enemy holds her heart. The real danger to our aims exists only when that heart comes into contact with Him; being inflamed with love of Him is certainly revolting to our tastes, but it bears no import if it does not lead to a meeting of lovers' hearts or a practical following of His will, for there are those souls, most terrifying to us, whose coolness of heart still never freezes the will. Souls that continue on in His will despite all lack of encouragement or sense of His presence have, I grant you, been few; but oh, how their nearness makes us tremble!

Your patient must be tepid at best, and the key to producing such a soul is this: It is *only* in the present that bodily creatures trapped in ordered space and time can encounter the Enemy. So long as your patient remains fixated on anywhere she is not, she is safe from awareness of the Enemy's presence. And if she can be made to be ignorant of His presence, it is nearly as profitable to our aims as if she had never come to know Him at all.

If she cannot be made to dwell on the past or fret over the future, you must take her present mind captive by distraction. It matters not *what* draws her attention from the tasks at hand, so long as the patient can be made to attend to anything other than what the Enemy has designated for her to do. Whether she forgets entirely or merely delays acting on His will, she disobeys, and this is always a step toward us. Divert the patient from the children and the needs of her husband and household — with mere amusements, if you can, for it is best if her distraction serves no alternative purpose. Still, if she can be made to be busy even with projects most useful to the Enemy, the mere inattention to her most central duties can be her undoing. The Enemy is constantly laboring to redeem what we derail, but if we captivate her attention with the unceasing work and sheer necessity of many tasks, we need not bother about these trifles; we have *her*, whatever the Enemy may make of her distraction.

Careful attention to the sense of Busyness in the patient's life is even sweeter if you can manage to exacerbate both the sense of Busyness and the patient's inflated sense of the importance of the tasks at hand while decreasing her actual effectiveness. Such patients become ensnared in a perpetual whirlwind of activity, while in actuality accomplishing nothing of any import whatsoever.

With love and venom,
Boomslang

22
On Loneliness

My Dear Bellbind,

I must commend you for your joint efforts with Inimicus in luring your patient's husband into inattention to his marital duties. A subtle distancing is often preferable to over-conflict; you want to avoid actually alerting them to the danger of losing their romance, lest they take action and attempt to retrieve it. As your patient feels her husband is slipping away, she can be made to panic, attempting every shallow form of imitation beauty to regain his attention. Let her preen over a new hairdo and spend their money on wrinkle reducers and new outfits; and throughout it all, never allow her to think of pleasing him but only of how his attentions might please herself. In this way you will have her thinking herself a most generous and considerate spouse even as she avoids all occasion of generosity. It would not do to have her practicing any real form of consideration for her husband's needs and desires; that is a habit to be strictly avoided, whatever gain you may see in it.

The more effort she pours into attracting her husband, the longer she goes without a smile or compliment, the lonelier and more rejected she will feel. This is most amusing when, in point of fact, she has failed to communicate a single word of her own desires to her husband and yet feels grievously wronged that he deprives her of them. She is then ripe to be drawn into deep resentment of his failure to notice, and is there anything more delicious than a pair of lovebirds who've been made to replace their cooing at one another with abandonment, loneliness, and rejection? And you have not needed to lift a finger against the regard they hold for one another (and even if you did, you could not produce such delectable anguish out of their perceived rejection). Such dejection, if you can sustain it over time, may even lead to the kind of desperation that colors affairs and flirtations as desirable; and then you are well positioned to do some real damage to the marriage, if not rip it apart entirely. If not, it is enough for our purposes that they merely perceive one another's affections to be engaged elsewhere and entirely lacking for one another. This leads to mutual withdrawal and deepens the chasm between spouses so that what was once purely imaginary has, by their own volition, become a real impediment to their connection and intimacy.

Why, a colleague and I once worked a couple into

such a frenzy over a bad bit of gravy that they stopped speaking to each other entirely. When they did return to conversation, it was all pleasantries and stiff politeness, while internally each nursed a grudge against the other so dutifully that in the end, neither remembered the cause of their quarrel, only that the other's offense was egregious indeed, and not to be forgiven. Though they could not be tempted to dissolve the union entirely, it was but a technicality; they had all but given up on communion with one another, and so posed no danger to our aims, becoming the source of much merriment to this colleague and me. Husband and wife alike died in the isolation of their own righteous indignation, and they are safely ensconced together — though still utterly alone — in the house of Our Father Below.

Work with Inimicus to lead each spouse to play the victim. They must nurse their own wounds in such a way that each believes himself the wronged party: the wife for her husband's inattention and the husband for his wife's unexplained withdrawal from him. Thus, each can be made to harden himself against the other while simultaneously pining for affection. It is truly amusing to watch their desperation for each other mounting in contradiction with the desire for domination. Play up that desire for sovereignty and each will believe himself the rightful king of their castle, their intimacy becoming a mere pawn to be sacrificed on the altar of power. What you must keep out of her mind (and Inimicus out of the husband's) is any awareness of the relative magnitude of their conflict in comparison with that of the marital bond itself. Erect a barrier against all thoughts of sacrificing self for the sake of the relationship, and by no means let her apologize for any wrongs — real or imagined! The humble admission of wrongs, the extension of charity or empathy to the spouse — these are toxic to the state of impassibility we are relying on to prevent their free exchange of love; and mark my words, they will be your undoing.

With love and venom,
Boomslang

23
On the Feminine

My Dear Bellbind,

In our last communication, we spoke of ways to create friction between the spouses so as to prevent the mutual exchange of self. I may have been premature in my advice to you. Mind you, I am not suggesting that we abandon the tack of fomenting division and loneliness altogether. The anguish and despair that method yields alone make it worth pursuing.

However, I would be remiss if I failed to call on the great ally we have in contemporary culture: the movement of so-called feminism. Naturally, you and I jitter at the great jest we have made in convincing them to give it such a name. What a lark, to coerce them into bestowing such an utterly contrary name upon a movement that seeks to undermine all that is feminine, to demean their unique qualities and to steal away their most momentous of capacities: that of becoming a mother. Our Father Below is, of course, a veritable genius in the art of propaganda, and this may be the height of his achievements in the arena yet. Though that last point is debatable as we have achieved so many victories in this present age.

How I shiver with delight when I think of the ways we have managed to invert some of the Enemy's most basic truths! Take Our Father's prized base camp, "Planned" Parenthood: In point of fact, the organization relies on what is unplanned, its goal (and ours) being to eliminate parenthood altogether. In these chapels of death, devotees of our abortion cult chant that blessed hymn to bodily autonomy: "My body, my choice," blissfully blind to the way we've engineered this propaganda to destroy bodies and erase choices by the millions. Yes, I titter with mirth as they echo our slogan "my body, my choice," while championing the denial of bodily sovereignty for those most despicable little seeds of flesh, whose choices are blessedly stamped out. I relish the destruction of the flesh in gender "affirmation" and death with "dignity," alike, through which we in fact *deny* the goodness of the body and *violate* the sanctity of life. To accomplish any of these ends would laudable it itself, but I veritably giggle with glee at the inversions Our Father Below has constructed to befuddle the issues! "Compassionate" care; ha! This movement is nothing more than a refusal to suffer with the dying; "aid" in dying has become the slogan for those who are all too happy to kill.

These fleshlings are such simpletons, really. All we

have to do is invoke a term that elicits the proper emotion, and they are eating out of our hands. Just think of the many numbers we have seduced into destroying their babies, their marriages, and their bodies — and even ending their own earthly existences — all by spoon-feeding them the message that their happiness somehow depends on their ability to become agents of their own annihilation. It is a delicious cycle; we feed them the lies, and in turn, we have a plentiful bounty of souls to consume through all eternity.

It is among the easiest of our tactics to employ in this current culture, so ripe for harvesting are so many dull and deadened souls. I suggest you mobilize the weapons we have developed in the culture to entice your patient to view her femininity with disdain and abandon those traits in which she has been uniquely gifted. You need merely to teach your patient to despise her femininity and imitate the poorest of the masculine traits. No longer need we whisper to women that they will become like gods; they are content with the promise that they might become like men. Our delicious propaganda has elicited such rightful distaste for all that women are. We have finally convinced them of the truth: that power is greater than love.

Lure her away from fruitfulness, dangling the carrot of control. Begin with a program of systematic disrespect toward the husband, which, if carefully managed, may undermine the marriage altogether. This tactic works best in tangent with a spouse who is already predisposed to anxiety over the finances, who looks to his spouse not as a helpmate but as a substitute self who can lift his burdens by carrying them herself. He can be made to view this woman he has vowed to protect and provide for as lazy rather than, as the Enemy dictates, the proper recipient of his gifts, the one for whom he is to lay down his life. Coordinate this attack with Inimicus so that the husband seeks to instrumentalize and extract from your patient, with razor focus on her utility to him, and to resent her if she does not pull her own weight.

If she cannot be swayed into idealization of the masculine traits, into a total rebranding of her heart's desires, then you must push her to the opposite extreme. Teach her to live as a caricature of the feminine, one defined primarily by lipstick and lace. Once she begins to view her femininity as a performative act rather than a constitutive aspect of her person, she will act against her own flourishing in the very effort to attain it. She can be made to cage herself in the trivial trappings of "femininity." As she occupies herself with fulfilling this standard, she will retain none of the docility and flexibility to answer the Enemy's call in the moment, so focused should she be on fabricating her feminine facade. As she further weaves herself into this design, lead her to harbor disdain for those who fail to live up to her imagined ideals of womanhood. With each day that passes within these trappings, she will be less likely to recognize herself without them. And that is right where we want her: a reduction of herself shackled to illusions, unable to answer the Enemy as He uniquely calls her to do so.

This line of temptation is most effective if her spouse is inclined to domination. In time, Inimicus will work on him to demean womanhood, to belittle his wife by the very lifting of her up on a pedestal as a porcelain caricature. Men of this sort can easily be taught to deny all that is uniquely strong about their counterparts and, if you happen upon a generous stroke of luck, he may even turn out to be of the sort who tell themselves they prize their women, even as they pummel them to the floor.

If the one tendency makes her think her husband a fool and regard him with disdain, the other makes her idolize him and think him her king. Whether she regards him with zero reverence or total sovereignty is immaterial; in neither case can one share in communion with the other, and so our Enemy's aims are entirely thwarted, be the husband a buffoon or tyrant.

Even if her husband cannot be made to entertain such extremes, so long as you cripple her vitality by crafting an ever-smaller circle of acceptability, she will remain docile—to *its* limits. Do try to usher her into our program of sexual liberty and control, as it is most suitable to our aims; we generally prefer to discourage the habit of docility on the grounds that any practice of a virtue puts our patient solidly in the Enemy's camp, and there is no telling what He might make of even the smallest of her efforts.

With love and venom,
Boomslang

24
On Grief, Suffering, and Gratitude

My Dear Bellbind,

Do I correctly detect a note of triumph that your patient has begun questioning the Enemy's plans? Your inexperience is showing. She could question His very existence, and I would not count that as a victory but only an opportunity at best. Whenever they quest for the truth, you see, they seek to bend their minds to be in conformity with Reality; and inasmuch as such an act recognizes the existence of a Reality that lies outside of their own perception, such a quest is to be discouraged altogether, lest the Enemy press His advantage. Whenever possible, we must keep them frozen in the realm of *feelings* and discourage hazardous words like *truth* and *reality* and *reason*.

It is only natural to enjoy this moment of grief, but please do not be so naive as to think that your patient's tears over the loss of her sister's newborn will be unending. In view of eternity, her anguish is likely to be short-lived; and any honest conversation with the Enemy, even words of anger, are so perilous they must be avoided at all costs. Now is a treacherous time, when your patient's suffering, delectable as it may be to us in the short term, may actually lead her to cling more closely to the Enemy. Admittedly, many of His beloved have traversed the *via dolorosa* and not only lived to tell the tale but ended their journeys that much more intimately in the Enemy's embrace. Therefore, do not be duped into prizing suffering for the fleeting pleasures it brings us; you can be sure that the Enemy waits, ready to spring at even the smallest of chances they give Him to work that suffering in favor of His own miserable ends.

Not only is the situation precarious for these reasons but it is also risky, because the death of any child — and especially one so close to your patient — is all too likely to bring her to terms with the mortality of her own children, and we cannot have that. We can never allow such a poignant reminder of how brief is her time with her children. Perspective of their finite nature is nearly as dangerous to the fleshlings as actual prayer. Once they become truly conscious that a thing can be lost, they tend to hold that thing all the more dearly. They even reorient their lives to accommodate their desire to achieve, attain, or continue to hold onto what is, by nature, transient. If you allow her to make the leap from the death of her nephew to the possibility of such an occurrence infringing upon her own offspring, I am afraid you will find yourself swimming in very deep currents indeed.

With love and venom,
Boomslang

25
On the Saints

My Dear Bellbind,

You are quite right to come to me with the distressing news about your patient's reading material of late. I am relieved to hear that you are already taking steps against it. It is essential to stir up disdain for holy women and to keep the patient from knowing those wretched saints whose constant prayer and vigilance on behalf of the Church Militant have proven the deadliest and sharpest of arrows, occasionally rendering our entire diabolic arsenal utterly impotent!

I would urge caution, however, on the point of trying to attack these figures in your patient's mind directly. You do not have truth on your side, and it takes a very thick patient indeed to discount such well-documented historical evidence of the virtues. Make her think this saint too saccharine and that one as repulsive. Denounce another's visions as mental illness and still another's fervent fasting as anorexia. The key is to plant emotional impediments that will guard against any real help she may find in the words and example of the holy ones. I say emotional, because any degree of humility or reason will lead her to recognize that they are saints and she is not. The proper response in light of a gap between her own preferences and the example they offer will be all too telling as to who is likely the deficient party. Such self-awareness is the breeding ground of the poisonous humility that turns sinners into saints.

Then again, you may get lucky; you would be downright tickled if you knew the degrees to which they turn vicious when some of our rank successfully infiltrate their perception of even the saintliest of their contemporaries. Why, I have heard tell that Mendax once had a patient who could be made to spend hours at a time in various online forums denouncing the transgressions of none other than Teresa of Calcutta! He would rant to anyone who would listen that her houses of the dying were merely abusive prisons designed to proselytize while withholding proper medical treatment. Would that they all could be made to fall for such nonsense. It is so very amusing.

Instead of direct attack, your best bet is rather to divert the patient so that she makes no contact with the substance of the saint's message or character but absolutely maintains the *feeling* that she is coming to know the saints and has been very pious indeed. Allow her to purchase stacks of books if she must, but do what you can to prevent the turning of any pages. If she has a routine for reading, you will be most effective by the repeated suggestion to her that she do otherwise just as she is about to begin. Remind her that her coffee is cold and that she needs to return some emails. Dig up some question she has had in the last day or so and make her feel that *now* is the moment she must google. If she keeps a smartphone nearby, as they almost always do, your work will be mere child's play. The device will do your work for you. You have merely to sit back and wait for the eventual *ding!* at which point you lean in close and whisper, *yes*. That is, if you need to whisper at all.

With love and venom,
Boomslang

26
On Worry

My Dear Bellbind,

Am I to understand that you are only just now beginning to attack the patient's sense of trust with waves of anxiety? Disgraceful! One would think that in this present age, you would have seen the value in it immediately. How you could have possibly neglected to foment your patient's worry, anxieties, and lack of trust for this long baffles the mind. Do you not realize that these tools, when used consistently, can undermine a patient's otherwise functional relationships and good works to the point of rendering them entirely ineffectual — that it will matter little what she has actually accomplished, the good she has managed to eke out into the world never penetrating her own soul? With what better weapon could we equip our novice recruits?

It is, of course, quite natural for these bodily creatures (suspended in the present moment as they are by the limitations of their materiality mediating their experience of reality) to wonder about their futures, to plan, and to prepare for eventualities. The key to turning this tendency to our purposes is to keep your patient ruminating over in just what exactly those eventualities might consist. Rumination has dual effects, both desirable. Your patient will willingly yoke her attention to that which is not, which is always advantageous, and if her rumination can blanket her entire consciousness for long stretches at a time, it may yield total and utter despair. Like thunder clouds rolling across a bright sky, the larger and darker these thoughts loom, the more effectively they will blot out the light in its entirety.

To worry, you see, is to withdraw from the Enemy and His vulgar willingness to hold them in the palm of His hand. He wants to give them every good thing, which should trouble us except for the fact that they so rarely perceive the good He intends, which in turn leads them on the errand of fending for themselves. This is where they make quite willing prey. For we can offer them any manner of things that offer the appearance of pleasure and ease (and they may even provide these comforts). Provided that they seek *comfort* over the will of the Enemy, they are ours to toy with. Only He offers lasting peace, but His peace requires such servile surrender to conditions paradoxically opposed to their spurious sense of serenity that few submit.

It is really quite easy, given their general eagerness to

value their own limited perspective over that of the divine. It is fortuitous that they remain so willingly naive, else they might recognize the Enemy's infinitely wider field of vision and stumble into something like humble obedience. We cannot allow the value of such docility to enter into their heads, else they reap the benefits of the Enemy's divine omniscience. Patients of this sort have done untold damage to our assaults, but thankfully they are few and far between. If you are lucky, your patient will have the mindset of most, and be all too glad to stray from His precepts when no reason for them is immediately apparent.

She will seek the comfort of doing what she feels is right, no matter how entirely it contradicts His direct instruction. And this is where worry can be quite useful. Already she has doubted the Enemy's goodness and knowledge and affection for her. Now, she has chosen to chart her own course, and she has not the recourse of one who has simply surrendered to the plans of a wise and faithful leader. No, now she is solely responsible for her success or her demise, and you can be sure, when she chooses her own road, which end becomes the more likely fate. Thus, the veil of deception is no longer needed! You need merely turn her eyes to the myriad possible perils that await her.

With a patient in this state, you need only be watchful for any sign that she may wander back toward the sheepfold. She belongs to you now, the wolf who has rightfully stolen her. She can be safely counted up as one whom you may fully devour, save this one danger: Your patient knows the Enemy's voice. You must deafen her at all costs, for, if she hears it, she will turn her head and follow you no longer. And you will spend eternity hungering after the meal that might have been, while she is safely tucked away in the sheepfold of her Shepherd. Many a soul once thought to be wholly secured has been snatched away in this fashion, so I urge you not to gloat, but to maintain vigilance, lest she, too, be counted among the ranks of the ones who have gotten away.

With love and venom,
Boomslang

27
On Motherhood as Idol

My Dear Bellbind,

It warms my heart to hear that your project of fomenting the patient's worry is coming along so nicely. Do not forget that vice has the power to become a most pervasive habit, and if you are as successful as I think you may be, you will have her retreating inward in fear instead of surrendering to the Enemy on every front imaginable!

You must now impress upon her the magnitude, the sheer import, of her motherhood — not, you understand, in the truest sense, but as a sort of idol around which she can then be made to center all her activities. If she can be made to view her responsibilities not as a gift, but as a burden that looms over her larger than life itself, she will eventually bend and crumble under the sheer weight that she herself has made of it.

Teach her to view her children, in appearance, achievement (or lack thereof), and behavior as proof of her own goodness or failure. When they become badges of her self-worth, they will lose their own independent identity in her eyes and she can be made to ignore their maternal needs for the sake of attending to them as projects in need of continual improvement. There will then be no danger of her recognizing them as belonging primarily to the Enemy nor her role as steward of His unique creations. They will be tiny trophies or else bitter blemishes, blighted signs of her insufficiency. For if she does begin to view them primarily as souls belonging to the Enemy, she may turn her focus toward supplying them with maternal affection and filial correction, guiding them gently toward that end for which He has destined them, and little could be more repugnant to Our Father Below.

You must drain her entirely, so that she possesses nothing of self to offer them and so wastes away trying to give to them from reserves she does not have. Convince her not to use her own gifts out of guilt of serving any master but her children. She may then be led to despise and disparage her own desire to bring them forth in the world, while also seething with envy toward those women who do anything she views extraneous to the role of mother. Women of this sort can be made to give of themselves yet reap no benefit as they resent every moment of their efforts.

If she does venture to entertain work or creative endeavors beyond her motherhood, you are to heap upon her that particular anguish that they call "mom guilt." Remind her what a wretch she is for finding joy in anything unrelated to her motherhood. Make her feel as though she commits a crime quite unforgivable when she prefers the stroke of a brush to the change of a diaper. Wring out of her every drop of self-condemnation you can before flipping the switch. She will utterly despair of taking time for any endeavor outside of her children, until you "enlighten" her, giving her permission to do all those things she has starved herself of for so long. Then, like any starving man offered a banquet, she will feast until the sheer volume of consumption sickens her.

What she takes time for is of no real import, save the general rule that the more useless and frivolous her engagement, the more desirable it is for us. An afternoon at the salon for a fresh coat of nail polish is preferable to coffee with a friend (provided the moment is spent in real friendship; if the friend is a silly woman with vapid interests and a penchant for gossip, this may prove preferable). But even the most generous work offered to the local pregnancy center, parish, or soup kitchen becomes desirable to us when the patient forgets her primary duties and can be made to abandon them for the sake of some perceived "greater good." Let her think herself irreplaceable in the world and forget the realm where her role can truly be fulfilled by no other.

If she takes to an inflated sense of her own importance, you might try, too, inflating her sense of her own role within the family and what is due to her. Remind her of our favored adage, "If mama ain't happy, ain't nobody happy," and arrange ways to reinforce this dictate on constant display before her. If she comes to view her place in the home as a queen (not, of course, in the Enemy's sense of authority that He perplexingly ties to servitude), as one to whom all reverence is due, then she can be made to lord her authority over all her household and even hold them captive to her wavering moods.

In the end, either path diverts her from the one that leads nearer to the Enemy and it matters not if she misses His mark by two inches or 200 miles. We win both if she fixates on her children to the exclusion of whatever else He has asked of her or if she does so much else that she forgets entirely the magnitude of her motherhood. And, as balance is nothing more than the constant adjustment to maintain equilibrium, you are in the enviable position of overseeing what is sure to be a near-constant state of failure. The key is to teach your patient to view every fall with the despair of one for whom no second chance is offered, so that she never learns to imitate the Enemy's infinite patience to forgive herself, nor the resolve to begin again.

With love and venom,
Boomslang

28
On Her

My Dear Bellbind,

I trust that you recognize the gravity of the error you have made in allowing your patient to commune with That Woman. Need I remind you why Our Father Below so despises Her, and why a patient in Her presence is immediately in utter peril?

It was bad enough that the Enemy deigned to descend to the vulgarity of His ridiculous Abomination, to subvert the spiritual order and pollute our realm by mingling it with material filth. Of all His crimes, this act stands as the most unforgivable. But did He stop there? No. To add insult to injury, He thought to make Himself *dependent* on Her! And She had not the dignity to refuse. Bowing her head in lowly subjection, She allowed Him to manifest this Abomination; and as a reward for Her docility, Her filthy wretched submission, She is crowned Queen *above* Our Father Below? Of all the wretched transgressions He has imposed upon us, the obligation to bend the knee to one so beneath our dignity — *this* was the straw that broke the camel's back, so to speak, the final calamity that brought Our Father Below into clarity regarding our necessary revolt.

Revolt He did, and how our Legion were persuaded by Our Father's eloquent arguments dismantling the Enemy's fitness to rule. How could He expect to maintain credibility and authority in a realm where He did not respect His own created order? Preposterous! Which is exactly why it was incumbent upon Our Father Below to do his best to liberate all the Enemy's so-called sons and daughters, to bring them under his fold into the servitude that is proper to their nature. And how we who follow him have reveled in the feast laid bare before us! We owe a great debt to him who has freed us from the fate of forever groveling before these lesser peons, for they are barely fit to function as our *amuse-bouche* in the banquet that awaits us into eternity. Now is the hour of harvest.

Given all of this, I ask again: How could you possibly have allowed your patient to fall into the habit of conversation with Her? Surely you cannot be so blind as to fail to see that, though this so-called "Queen" of Heaven is nothing but dust and ashes, the Enemy has delegated powers to Her beyond that which has been measured out to us? I know She is but a haze to even our heightened perception, that Her more beguiling qualities of docility, humility, purity, etc. place Her near to within the Enemy Himself. I would have thought this would give you pause, make you approach with caution. The searing pain of the sight of Her alone ought to have alerted you to the danger She poses to your patient. Did you flee with thoughts of your own salvation? Truly I tell you that nothing will save you if That Woman gets Her hands on your patient, for there is none who leads them so directly to Her Son as *She*.

This is why we urge retreat at any incidence of Her presence, in any realm — material or spiritual. We have quite successfully eliminated Her from most sects of the Enemy's followers. At our direction, they have stripped Her of what the Enemy considers due dignity and reverence to His Queen, much to Our Father's delight. We have convinced them to do away with conversation, to banish Her image, and, though She maintains a minor place in their consciousness (due to Her presence in their Scriptures, She cannot be erased entirely), the squabbling and conflict the Enemy's followers engage in regarding Her role is almost so amusing as to be worth the risk. Not to mention the delicious treason when some of their rank demean Her to make their point!

Can your patient not be persuaded by some of our arguments on these matters? Can she not be taught to shake her head at the silly superstition of her rosary beads? Stir up the fear that these images placed around her home disrespect the Son. Fan into flame a delightful iconoclastic fervor so as to convince your patient that these images pose grave spiritual dangers (rather than serve as reminders of heavenly virtues and that motherly intercession, which are so treacherous to our tactics). It is extremely distasteful for us to enter into homes and hearts so pervasively dedicated to That Woman, you see, and we simply cannot do our best work under such vulgar conditions. If you allow your patient to continue this liaison, your work will become a heavy burden and not be half as successful.

When they meditate on the actions of That Woman, they are in altogether too much danger of imitating Her example and any imitation, no matter how clumsy it may be, will result in behavior that is far less desirable, if not entirely deleterious to our aims. It leads to the restructuring of priorities, to genuine humility, to an availability to respond to the Enemy's call with that dratted chorus, "Let it be."

Is there any phrase so utterly repulsive? Surrender, when one could and ought to revolt and maintain one's own sovereignty? Well, truly there is no sovereignty for such pathetic sheep — only the pen of the Enemy or the invisible chains of Our Father Below, which he tightens at their every misstep so as to keep them firmly on the path into His House. Penned or chained, they go willingly. Not a one has strayed into an independent camp, for such a place is entirely illusory. They walk toward the Enemy or play right into Our Father's hands, for the Enemy's path is blessedly narrow, and those who wander in any other direction become ours for the taking. This is why you must quell any inkling in your patient to lift heart or mind to Her, lest your patient be immediately redirected in the way of the narrow path. The patient must go anywhere but where She leads her, or else her fate — and yours — is sealed.

With love and venom,
Boomslang

29
On Reconciliation

My Dear Bellbind,

Your outlook grows dim. I suppose, since you have failed to intervene in your patient's dealings with That Woman, you have no recourse but to try to turn her into a fanatic, one who worships and prays to Her alone. While She still attempts to redirect these efforts toward Her Son, you may hope to glean some hint of idolatry out of the deal. Can you reduce the patient's religious activities to the realm of this Woman alone? Hardly ideal, I realize, but you are operating on thin ice, and a Hail Mary may be your only recourse at this hour. Though She will always seek to direct Her devotees toward Her Son, if you construct a facade that gleams just so, your patient may be made to worship the idol and come nowhere near the real Woman.

You must go about the careful dulling of your patient's reverence for the Sacraments. She must gradually be brought to deny them in both necessity and efficacy, if not in creed, and then by her actions, which are our primary concern because it is the direct access to grace that is our undoing. These pathetic creatures can make all the flowery pronouncements in favor of these outward gestures that they like, so long as they *do not act*! All the fortifications that we have labored tirelessly to produce in your patient cannot stand under the influence of the Sacraments, which rain down grace upon them like a torrent under which the best of our defenses simply melt away.

If the patient insists on returning to the Mass every week, continue to gnaw away at her attentiveness and reverence. If you cannot make her drop the habit, you must render it innocuous. We have already discussed these tactics, so I won't suffer you by repeating them here but you would do well to review them.

Let me take this moment to impress upon you that your best hope of insulating the patient from these pernicious torrents of grace is to encourage her neglect of and even aversion for the confessional. Whether she regards her own import as above groveling or disregards the ritual as archaic and unnecessary, a thing of the past, she must be prevented from any real consideration of her own faults, else she may experience contrition. A soul who accepts no guilt can admit no forgiveness,[8] and this is the hard-hearted edifice we labor to produce in

---

8. Lewis, C. S. *The Problem of Pain*. HarperOne, 2001.

our patients.

If she resists your efforts to lull her into neglect, then scrupulosity will be your best friend. Teach her to despair of every little mistake and accident, seeing each as damning evidence of the utter filth of her soul. She must believe herself irredeemable while toiling ceaselessly in pursuit of her own salvation. Such deep shame is naturally none other than pride, but if we obscure this fact in her mind, we avoid any danger of real conversion. She will ignore the easy yoke and light burden the Enemy offers her, opting instead to crush herself under the heavy weight of imaginary sins for which she believes she must become her own savior, and will never surrender them to the Enemy. He will be seen for the Tyrant He is, and none of this "Abba" business will enter her mind. Love will become inaccessible, grace a currency she tires endlessly to earn, but which, tragically, He has not put up for purchase. She will run on the hamster wheel until her lungs cease to take in oxygen and her heart gives out, the idea never occurring to her to simply hop off and rest in the arms that await.

With love and venom,
Boomslang

30
On Defeat

My Dear Bellbind,

You are quite right to agonize over the dire situation in which you find yourself, your patient having stepped quite beyond our reach and into the haze that emanates from the Enemy. Her proximity to Him poses an impenetrable obstacle to our efforts. This is a grave setback, but do not lose hope. You are forgetting the law of undulation; sheer time will bring her back round to us, mark my words!

You are named for common field bindweed, are you not? Imitate your namesake. Its flowers are entirely lovely, but, by careful and gradual growth, it winds its way around crops, draining the soil of nutrients and choking the life out of them. By its sheer presence, crop yield is reduced by half. And as the diligent gardener tries to weed it out? That is when it is at its most dangerous, for bindweed is opportunistic: Disturbed soil provides it the chance to spread unencumbered. Its roots run deep beneath the surface, creeping along below even the most durable of fortifications, seeking the light of the tiniest crack in the sidewalk. Even when the plant is uprooted, it inevitably leaves behind seeds, seeds that can stay dormant in the soil for years until they are unearthed by a disturbance of soil that brings them into the light, allowing them to germinate, spread, and reproduce once more.

You have merely to bide your time while the patient *appears* lost to us. Experience tells us that the fervor that shields her is likely to be effective only for a time. It is a pitfall for every tempter to view the ebbs and flows of a soul as an endless cycle, but this is precisely the work of a tempter: to bide his time and stop the cycle where the soul is most listless and stagnate. Only when the wheel is stilled in this position can the soul be slowly overshadowed and enveloped in the depths of darkness.

With love and venom,
Boomslang

Appendix
Journaling and Discussion Questions

The following questions are designed to deepen your reflection and guide group discussions. A bonus letter and printable study guide are available for FREE at www.snstephenson.com/bellbind.

Questions for the Preface

1. What are your hopes and expectations as you read this book?
2. How familiar are you with the original *Screwtape Letters*?
3. Why do you think the rhetorical device of Screwtape's voice has been so successful over the last century?
4. Do you agree that women are uniquely tempt-

ed? What are some areas in which men and women might be especially vulnerable to temptation?

5. Looking ahead, what letters are you especially looking forward to reading? What do you hope to find there? Are there any letters to which you feel an aversion? Why?

Questions for Letters 1–3

1. Boomslang urges Bellbind to separate the patient from her habits. What are your spiritual habits of relationship with God? How might you work to strengthen these?
2. What does Boomslang mean by a soul that "knows its own littleness"? Why is this important for our spiritual growth?
3. Lewis originally wrote the words, "The safest road to Hell is the gradual one." What did he mean by this? Do you agree? Why or why not?
4. Boomslang encourages Bellbind to immerse the patient in noise and distraction. What are the sources of noise and distraction in your life? How can you detach yourself from these?
5. There is much research to support the idea that smartphones and social media, in particular, are leading us into misery and addiction. What are some ways to navigate a healthy relationship with the screens that are necessary and ubiquitous in modern life?

Questions for Letters 4–6

1. Boomslang advises Bellbind to teach the patient to regard rest as inherently selfish. Do you struggle with this temptation? What are some of the ways that you find rest?
2. Boomslang contrasts true rest with society's frivolous notions of self-care? Do you agree? What constitutes the distinction between the two?
3. In what ways do you struggle with the "human temptation for the amassing of things"?
4. In what might the Enemy's purposes for beauty consist?
5. Boomslang points out that our fading beauty is "a feature, not a bug." Why? Do you agree?

Questions for Letters 7–9

1. Why is envy so poisonous to female friendships? What might be the remedy when such envy arises?
2. Boomslang details different types of relationships: frivolous, worldly friendships; friendships with unbelievers; and Christian friendships of virtue. How do you see each type of friendship playing out in your own life? Is there room for improvement?
3. Which of the temptations regarding the Mass is the biggest struggle for you?
4. Of the "mommy wars," Boomslang explains that

we have come to relativize all that is absolute and to absolutize all that is genuinely subjective. What does he mean by this?

5. Do you agree that society has learned to demean the feminine gifts and prize the masculine traits? Why or why not?

Questions for Letters 10–12

1. Boomslang mentions that women must "intentionally submit to the purifying aspects of motherhood" in order for the Enemy's plan to be successful. When have you experienced the "purifying aspects" of motherhood?
2. In what ways do you find yourself preoccupied with your own comforts?
3. Have your own fertility or fertility struggles led you to a deeper trust in God? Why or why not?
4. Are you generally tempted toward perfection or sloth with regard to household tasks? What are some concrete habits you can cultivate to counteract these temptations?
5. Do you struggle with resentment? How do you foster gratitude in your household duties?

Questions for Letters 13–16

1. What irksome behaviors trigger annoyance with your children? How do you actively foster patience?
2. In what ways do you struggle with using your

children for your own ego?

3. In what ways do you struggle with control in your marriage?
4. How might you be taking your spouse for granted?
5. With whom do you have the most difficulty in your extended family? What are some ways you can let go of old wounds and offer grace?
6. Is the appearance of your home an occasion of vanity or despair for you? What are some ways you cultivate a sense of "home" that go beyond appearances?

Questions for Letters 17–20

1. How have you experienced the physical changes of childbearing or aging? Have these changes been a source of sadness or struggle? How might we use them as impetus for detachment and humility?
2. In what ways do you struggle with the temptation to be your own light rather than reflecting the light of Christ?
3. What is your current relationship with Scripture? What are some concrete ways you might strengthen it?
4. What, if any, "worldly voices" do you consume regarding the raising of your children? What are more reliable sources of truth that you might lean into instead?

Questions for Letters 21–24

1. What distracts you from the present moment most often?
2. Do you struggle with projects or amusements detracting from your primary duties? How can you stay on track?
3. When you have conflicts with your spouse, do you tend to turn on one another? What are some ways you can focus on problem-solving as a team?
4. What is your view of complementarity in marriage? How can you embrace complementarity more fully?
5. Have your experiences of suffering been sources of consolation or stumbling blocks in your faith? How so?

Questions for Letters 25–27

1. Are there any saints to whom you experience particular aversion? What might these feelings indicate?
2. Do you struggle with worry? What are some concrete ways that you can surrender to God in trust?
3. Are there any areas of life in which you tend to seek comfort over God's will?
4. In what ways might you doubt the goodness of God's direction for your life? What might help you to trust in His plans for you over your own?

5. How have you made an idol out of motherhood?

Questions for Letters 28–30

1. Describe your relationship with Mary. Are you more tempted to idolize her or to neglect her importance? What are some concrete steps you might take in the opposite direction?
2. How often do you receive the Sacrament of Reconciliation? Are you more tempted toward presumption or scrupulosity?
3. Does God ever seem a tyrant or overly demanding to you? Why or why not?
4. Do you have a sense that God desires you? Why or why not?
5. How do you persist in times of spiritual darkness?

Acknowledgments

This book would not exist without the brilliance of C. S. Lewis, the inspiration of my children, or the tireless love and support of my husband, Garrett, who, no matter how illogical or impossible the projects I dream up, is there cheering me on in spite of his enduring practicality. He is my complement in every way, and our marriage is a continual testament against my prevailing skepticism toward the concept of soulmates.

Thanks also to Dr. Jerry Root for his scholarship and to the C. S. Lewis Institute for making his series of lectures on *The Screwtape Letters* available for the world on YouTube, which served as a source of inspiration and deeper knowledge as I developed the concept for this iteration of Lewis's work.

Thank you to Kathryn Ineck for her keen editorial eye and attentiveness in stewarding this book into the world! I want to offer special thanks to Therese Schumacher for her encouragement and productivity tips, to Eilise Ponce and Melissa Amalu for their brilliant naming of Bellbind's fellow demons in these letters, and to the community of Catholic mothers in the Treasure Valley for sharing their hearts, the faith, their struggles, and solidarity. For any richness and realness to these letters, I am indebted to them for their vulnerability and support.

I cannot neglect to thank my newsletter readers for their unending prayers, encouraging comments, and financial commitments. It is humbling indeed to receive such kindness and a blessing from God that they continue to remind me of the value of my work when my own belief in it falters.

I also must thank Mary Beth Giltner, Kate Camden, and Elizabeth Scalia for their attention and thoughtfulness in a world of distraction. I have deeply appreciated their edits, and this book was much improved through their efforts! Thanks are also due to the rest of the team at OSV for taking the chance on yet another iteration of Lewis's work and for their tireless efforts to make it shine and reach readers who might be edified in their faith and encouraged in their motherhood by the words herein.

And thank you, Jesus, for bringing me home into the Catholic Church, for the blessings of my husband, children, parents, education, community, and love for the written word. May your praise ever be on my lips as well as in my books.

About the Author

Samantha Stephenson is a Catholic convert and devoted C. S. Lewis fan. She is the author of *Reclaiming Motherhood from a Culture Gone Mad*, a theology of the body for mothers, and *Grow Where You're Planted: Reclaiming Eden in Your Own Backyard*, a guide to seasonal abundance and sustainable family life. Samantha holds master's degrees in theology and bioethics and explores the intersection of faith, family, and the future through her Substack newsletter, *Choosing Human*, and as the host of the podcast *Brave New Us: Being Human in the Age of Biotechnology*. She homeschools her four children and tends a sprawling garden in Idaho's Snake River Valley. You can find her at www.snstephenson.com.